Up and Coming

A Play

Eric Chappell

A Samuel French Acting Edition

SAMUELFRENCH-LONDON.CO.UK
SAMUELFRENCH.COM

Copyright © 2001 by Eric Chappell Productions Ltd
All Rights Reserved

UP AND COMING is fully protected under the copyright laws of the British Commonwealth, including Canada, the United States of America, and all other countries of the Copyright Union. All rights, including professional and amateur stage productions, recitation, lecturing, public reading, motion picture, radio broadcasting, television and the rights of translation into foreign languages are strictly reserved.

ISBN 978-0-573-01953-1

www.samuelfrench-london.co.uk

www.samuelfrench.com

FOR AMATEUR PRODUCTION ENQUIRIES

UNITED KINGDOM AND WORLD EXCLUDING NORTH AMERICA

plays@SamuelFrench-London.co.uk

020 7255 4302/01

Each title is subject to availability from Samuel French, depending upon country of performance.

CAUTION: Professional and amateur producers are hereby warned that *UP AND COMING* is subject to a licensing fee. Publication of this play does not imply availability for performance. Both amateurs and professionals considering a production are strongly advised to apply to the appropriate agent before starting rehearsals, advertising, or booking a theatre. A licensing fee must be paid whether the title is presented for charity or gain and whether or not admission is charged.

The professional rights in this play are controlled by Samuel French Ltd, 52 Fitzroy Street, London, W1T 5JR.

No one shall make any changes in this title for the purpose of production. No part of this book may be reproduced, stored in a retrieval system, or transmitted in any form, by any means, now known or yet to be invented, including mechanical, electronic, photocopying, recording, videotaping, or otherwise, without the prior written permission of the publisher. No one shall upload this title, or part of this title, to any social media websites.

The right of Eric Chappell to be identified as author of this work has been asserted by him in accordance with Section 77 of the Copyright, Designs and Patents Act 1988

UP AND COMING

First presented at the Theatre Royal Windsor on 4th July 1989 under the title **UP AND RUNNING**, with the following cast:

Higgs	Tony Caunter
The Rt. Hon. Philip Conway MP	Keith Barron
Vicky	Susie Blake
Lorna Fiske	Bridget McConnell
The Rt. Hon. George Reynolds MP	Philip Madoc
Lionel Berryman MP	Peter Cellier
The Rt. Hon. John Henderson MP	Angus Mackay

Directed by Mark Piper
Designed by Alexander McPherson
Lighting by Matthew Evered

CHARACTERS

Higgs, security officer, mid-30s
The Rt. Hon. Philip Conway MP (Pip), Deputy Prime Minister, late 40s
Vicky, actress, late 20s
Lorna Fiske, Pip's assistant, mid-30s
The Rt. Hon. George Reynolds MP, Home Secretary, late 40s-early 50s
Lionel Berryman MP, 50s
The Rt. Hon. John Henderson MP, Prime Minister, 60s

The action of the play takes place in a suite in a south coast hotel

Time — the late twentieth century

SYNOPSIS OF SCENES

ACT I

SCENE 1	Late evening in October
SCENE 2	An hour later

ACT II

SCENE 1	An hour later
SCENE 2	Half an hour later

Also by Eric Chappell,
published by Samuel French Ltd

Haunted
Haywire
Heatstroke
It Can Damage Your Health
Natural Causes
Something's Burning
Theft

ACT I

Scene 1

An expensive hotel suite in a south coast resort. Late evening. October

Please refer to the set plan on p.68

The set consists of an L-shaped lounge L and DR, and a bedroom UR, the bedroom visible through a cutaway wall DS. There is a door between the lounge and bedroom DC at a right angle to the audience. US of this door, set into the dividing wall between the two rooms, is a closet, the door of which opens into the lounge; this door has a full-length mirror on the inside which faces DS when the door is open. US of the closet is a door leading into the bathroom; a second door leads from the bathroom into the bedroom. A door in the L wall of the lounge leads into a corridor; this door has a security chain on it. The lounge has french windows, UR, leading on to a balcony that faces the seafront. The french windows have heavy drapes and inner lace curtains

The rooms are decorated in Regency style. The lounge has in it a sofa, easy chairs, drinks cabinet, coffee table with ashtray, table lamps, etc. There are vases of flowers, including roses. A "Do Not Disturb" sign — in English, French and German — hangs from the doorknob. Around the corner of the L, DS and in front of the fourth wall of the bedroom, are a chair, and a desk with papers, a form, magazines, a telephone, a pad of paper, pens, etc. A red dispatch box stands on the floor by a second coffee table. The bedroom contains a divan bed with overhead drapes, and two bedside tables with lamps on them. There is a radio on one of the tables

When the CURTAIN *rises, the bedroom is in darkness except for a shaft of light coming through the half-open bathroom door. The lounge curtains are open; the room is illuminated by a table lamp and the occasional flash of a rocket against the night sky. Outside in the street there are sounds of a chanting, shouting mob accompanied by the occasional explosion of a firework*

We hear the voices of Higgs and Pip, off, and the outer door opens

The Light in the bathroom is extinguished

Higgs enters, the room key in his hand. He is a burly man in his mid-thirties, wearing a dark suit. He walks on the balls of his feet in an attempt at athletic grace but only succeeds in looking ponderous. He glances around the room and switches on the main light. During the following he puts the key on the desk

Higgs Right, sir.

Pip (Philip) Conway, Deputy Prime Minister and Leader of the House, enters. He is a man in his late forties, handsome and usually distinguished but at the moment his elegant suit and bowler hat are besmirched with eggs, flour and scraps of vegetable. He opens the closet door and studies himself grimly in the mirror. He removes his bowler hat, brushes it and hurls it into the closet. He removes a Brussels sprout from his top pocket, surveys his jacket and glares at Higgs

Higgs (*uneasily*) Sorry about that, sir.
Pip It's completely ruined.
Higgs Yes — it looks worse in the light.
Pip Of course it looks worse in the light! It's your job to protect me from these indignities, Higgs.
Higgs We should have had more men on. I didn't realize you were so unpopular.
Pip (*indignantly*) I'm not unpopular. Don't you read the papers?
Higgs Well, something must have upset them. What did you say?
Pip Well, all I said was ... Wait a minute. You were there, Higgs. Weren't you listening?
Higgs No, I couldn't listen to the speech — not and remain wide awake.
Pip (*suspiciously*) What? (*He removes his jacket during the following, revealing a pair of colourful braces*)
Higgs It was a situation that called for the utmost vigilance. I could feel the naked hatred in that hall.
Pip (*turning*) Naked hatred! I was invited to that meeting. Most of the young people there were from my own party.
Higgs (*darkly*) And what about the others — those out there?
Pip Students. East Sussex, I imagine. Protesting over grants. I'm not even Minister of Education, Higgs.
Higgs Yes, I realized they were students when that inflated condom floated down from the balcony. They get them free, did you know that? Easy come, easy go, I suppose.
Pip All I know is there was complete pandemonium.
Higgs And all it needed was one determined man behind that pandemonium and you could have been snuffed out like a candle. And where would I have been then?

Act I, Scene 1   3

Pip (*staring*) Where would you have been?
Higgs My career would have been in tatters.

During the following, Pip moves to the french windows in order to draw the curtains

Higgs moves to the bathroom door, pauses and then opens it abruptly

A shadowy figure — Vicky, an attractive blonde in her late twenties wearing a close fitting, belted raincoat — darts silently from the bathroom into the darkened bedroom

Higgs looks thoughtful for a moment and closes the bathroom door

Not with the lights on, sir!

Pip steps back quickly from the french windows. Higgs switches off the main lights, draws the curtains and switches the lights on again

After all, we don't know who's out there.
Pip You mean the determined man?
Higgs Sitting there with a telescopic rifle and night sights. And some of those boys could shoot the pips out of a playing card. That's why you need protection.
Pip Higgs, you couldn't even protect me from a student with a bag of vegetables.
Higgs Don't remind me. When that first tomato struck I thought, "My God! That could have been a grenade." (*He moves to the bedroom door and listens at it, then opens it abruptly and peers in*)

Vicky flits back into the bathroom

Higgs closes the door

Pip What is it, Higgs? Why this excessive caution?
Higgs Just let's say we have additional cause for concern ...
Pip Of course! It's the Prime Minister, isn't it? He's in the room below. I knew I should have booked into another hotel. A recent poll had him down as the most hated prime minister of the last fifty years. And you don't stand next to an oak tree when there's lightning about.
Higgs It's not the Prime Minister, sir. In fact, that could be in our favour — at least we have more men on ... (*He heads for the bedroom*)

Pip, bewildered, follows Higgs. Vicky moves from the bathroom to the lounge, finally disappearing into the closet; the two men pursue the same course as far as the lounge without ever seeing her

Pip (*impatiently*) Higgs, what is it? What is this additional cause?
Higgs We've been handed certain letters — threatening your life.
Pip I'm a public figure. I'm used to those.
Higgs These are different. Apart from making vicious threats against your person, they also reveal a knowledge of your movements and intimate details of your personal life ...
Pip Intimate details. Who gave you these letters?
Higgs Your secretary.
Pip Why didn't she show them to me?
Higgs Perhaps she didn't wish to alarm you.
Pip I'm not alarmed. I don't scare easily. (*Pause*) Did you say vicious?
Higgs Blowing you away, splattering your brains over the wallpaper — that sort of thing.
Pip Oh. Probably some crank.
Higgs How do we know he's a crank? He could be a highly intelligent, civilized man.
Pip Civilized! He wants to blow me away; that's not civilized — that's murder.
Higgs Ah, but he wouldn't look upon it as murder — he'd look upon it as cleansing society.
Pip I don't see how splattering my brains over the wallpaper would cleanse society — and I don't think you should be quite so ready to accept his point of view. I must say you seem remarkably detached, Higgs. Whose side are you on?
Higgs Yours, sir.
Pip That's a relief.
Higgs We're in this together.
Pip Are we?
Higgs If your life is in danger it's my duty in the last resort to make the ultimate sacrifice.
Pip Ultimate sacrifice?
Higgs I'd have to throw you to the ground and cover you with my body.
Pip I didn't know that.
Higgs Part of the job.
Pip Ever done it before, Higgs?
Higgs No. Well, I wouldn't be here if I had, would I?
Pip No, I suppose not.
Higgs Something worrying you, sir?
Pip No, only I noticed you didn't get any tomato on you this evening ...

Higgs (*wincing*) I think I'd better check the back stairs — people have a habit of wandering through the kitchens ...
Pip I think we'd better stay fairly close tonight, Higgs. You can sleep on the couch.
Higgs Yes, sir — and not too much light. We don't want you silhouetted against the curtains. (*He dims the lights*) Do you want me to get you a sandwich, a salad or something?
Pip No, I think I've had enough salad for one evening, Higgs. I'm not really hungry.
Higgs (*moving to the door*) Right. When I return I'll knock four times. Two long — two short ... (*He demonstrates — with two short knocks and two long ones*)
Pip That was two short and two long, Higgs.
Higgs Was it? We'll keep it like that then. Don't want to confuse you ... (*He opens the door*)

Lorna Fiske enters the room carrying a sheaf of papers. She is a woman in her mid-thirties, fresh-faced, wearing glasses and with a severe hairstyle

Evening, miss.
Lorna Good-evening.

Higgs exits

He always looks at me as if he's planning a body search.
Pip (*suavely*) Can you blame him?
Lorna Oh, Pip. (*She pushes him playfully*)

Pip staggers backwards

Suppose someone heard?
Pip You're right, we must be careful — especially now. But it's damned difficult, Lorna.
Lorna (*dropping her eyes*) Is it?
Pip (*eagerly*) Is that the speech?
Lorna Yes — I've amended it to bring in the events of this evening. We can't pretend it didn't happen.
Pip (*frowning*) Do we have to mention this evening? I looked a complete idiot.
Lorna No, you didn't, Pip, because you kept your dignity. Even when that cabbage knocked you off your feet you never stopped smiling.
Pip I wasn't smiling inside. (*Pause*) I think I was set up, Lorna.

Lorna So do I. It was the Prime Minister's idea, wasn't it, for you to attend?
Pip Yes.
Lorna I think you've become too popular. Everyone's talking about you. Now Coupland wants to do an interview.
Pip (*surprised*) Coupland. But he doesn't like me — he's never liked me. He objects to my policies.
Lorna I didn't say it was going to be a friendly interview. You'll have to tread carefully. I've made a few notes. I said we'd need sight of the questions.
Pip I don't like it. He could still spring something on me.
Lorna You mean regarding the succession?

Pip puts a finger to his lips

Pip Walls have ears, Lorna. We must be discreet. I don't want to be seen reaching for the crown.
Lorna On the other hand, you mustn't be overtaken by events. You'll see I've paid tribute to John Henderson and his years of service.
Pip Good. It's important to emphasize the years. I assisted him from the platform today.
Lorna I saw you. It had a noticeable effect on the delegates.
Pip It had a noticeable effect on Henderson; he hates it when I take his arm.
Lorna Then be careful — we mustn't make him suspicious. You know how paranoid he's become.
Pip (*softly*) Don't worry, I intend to back quietly and unobtrusively into the leadership. Tomorrow's speech will mark the beginning of my campaign. Reynolds is coming to see me tonight.
Lorna Then I'll leave you with the speech. (*She gives Pip the papers and smiles*) I hate to be here when you read it — it makes me nervous. (*She moves to the door*)
Pip Lorna — why didn't you tell me about the threatening letters?
Lorna Oh, those. I didn't want to alarm you.
Pip At least I could have worn a bullet-proof vest.
Lorna No, it makes you look corpulent — and you sweat. I wanted you to look relaxed.
Pip Lorna, I could have been killed. Would that have been relaxed enough for you?
Lorna No-one's going to kill you, Pip. You have a date with destiny tonight.
Pip Do I?
Lorna (*moving to the french windows and opening the curtains slightly*) Come here.
Pip (*uneasily*) I don't think we should stand by the window, Lorna.
Lorna Look. There's a bonfire on the beach. They're burning an effigy of the Prime Minister.

Act I, Scene 1   7

Pip moves unwillingly to the french windows

Pip They're not using me for kindling, are they?
Lorna No, they love you. We all do.
Pip Somebody doesn't — so come away.
Lorna Nothing's going to happen to you tonight — nothing unpleasant, that is. (*She caresses her throat*) I don't know if it's because of the fire but I feel strangely excited tonight, Pip.
Pip (*uneasily*) Do you?
Lorna I believe fire can do that to people ...
Pip So I understand.
Lorna (*squeezing Pip's hand*) Don't worry. It's moments like this that I'm glad we've waited —— (*She lifts Pip's hand to her lips*) Coupland won't be able to embarrass you with any of those questions. You're above suspicion, Pip.
Pip And we have to keep it that way.
Lorna (*archly*) Then behave, Pip. (*She pulls her hand away as if it's Pip who's doing the holding*) I'll go and run some cold water over my wrists and try to remain calm. You'll let me know what you think of the speech. (*She moves to the outer door and pauses*) Oh, and wear those colourful braces tomorrow.
Pip (*frowning*) Do I have to?
Lorna Yes, everyone's talking about them. (*She blows him a kiss*)

Pip pretends to catch the kiss

Lorna exits

Pip studies the speech. At the same time he picks up his jacket and opens the closet door to hang it up. Vicky takes it from him; only her her hand is visible

Pip (*reading*) "This is the time to return to the frank, open face of government — not to serve vested interests but to involve all sections of society in our decision making ... "

Vicky hands Pip another jacket from the closet. Pip takes the jacket and then stares at the hand

   Vicky!

Vicky emerges from the closet

   What are you doing here? How did you get in?

Vicky A porter opened the door for me.
Pip But this place is subject to maximum security. The PM's in the suite below. There are police all round the building. I've a bodyguard who's showing distinct signs of becoming trigger happy. And you just walk in!

Vicky kisses Pip lightly on the lips

Vicky I got tired of waiting. You said we'd meet. You promised last week.
Pip A week's a long time in politics, Vicky. Things have changed. (*He slips on the jacket and studies his reflection*)
Vicky What do you mean?
Pip Vicky, I'm a cabinet minister — and I'm married.
Vicky That hasn't changed since last week.
Pip All right. We met at a couple of receptions. We held hands in a taxi. We kissed in your hallway.
Vicky Passionately.
Pip How passionately is immaterial. There's still time to draw back.
Vicky Do you want to draw back?
Pip (*after a hesitation*) I can't afford a breath of scandal — particularly at the moment.
Vicky I wouldn't embarrass you, Pip.
Pip You already have. You've been following me. You were in the Strangers' Gallery last week. When I rose to speak you leaned over so far I thought you were going to fall into my lap.
Vicky I don't suppose anyone noticed.
Pip Didn't they? Did you read Coupland's column last week? (*He snatches a paper from the pile on the desk and reads*) "When Philip Conway rose to speak, a beautiful blonde, sitting in the Strangers' Gallery, leaned forward, rested a delicate chin on her hand and listened in rapt attention. Conway certainly appeals to the ladies."
Vicky You certainly do. (*She takes the paper from him*) I like the "beautiful blonde ... delicate chin" bit. May I keep it? I don't get many good reviews.
Pip (*holding up a magazine*) You've also managed to appear in several official photographs. People will begin to think you're in the cabinet! (*He looks at her curiously*) How do you do it? How do you get into official receptions without an invitation?
Vicky (*shrugging*) It's the only way I can get to see you.
Pip Well, you can't stay here — it's too risky. (*Pause*) Why do you want to see me?
Vicky I love you.
Pip You can't — it's too sudden.
Vicky It was like a thunderbolt.
Pip (*flattered*) A thunderbolt? But you hardly know me.

Act I, Scene 1

Vicky At first sight.
Pip Well, you can't stay. I'll check the corridor. If anyone stops you, say you lost your way ... (*He moves to the door*)
Vicky Do you know what I'm wearing under my coat?
Pip (*turning*) No, I don't know what you're wearing under your coat and I don't care. (*He pauses*) I suppose it's something exotic.
Vicky You could say that.
Pip (*returning to where Vicky is standing*) Vicky, do you know how long it took me to get adopted? Seven years.
Vicky Poor Pip. What happened to your parents?
Pip Will you listen? Seven years getting adopted; ten years on the back benches; six years in cabinet; two years Deputy Leader. I can't risk all that. (*He pauses*) Is it something in lace?
Vicky No.
Pip Listen, there's a baying mob outside. I have a bodyguard on the stairs who's like a coiled spring. (*Pause*) Black chiffon?
Vicky No.
Pip Vicky, I may be receiving a visit from a senior colleague later tonight. The world's press is downstairs. I can't ... A basque and suspenders?
Vicky No; should I show you?
Pip No! I don't want you to show me. My secretary could be back at any moment.
Vicky Nothing.
Pip What was that?
Vicky Nothing — under my coat.
Pip (*appalled*) Nothing! You came through the streets like that? Suppose you'd had an accident. Why are you doing this?
Vicky (*shrugging*) You wouldn't come to see me — so I came to see you.
Pip I've been too busy to go to the theatre, Vicky.
Vicky You'd like the play. It's called "Run for Your Knickers". I play this scantily-clad girl trapped in a married man's bedroom.
Pip I don't need to go to the Pier Theatre for that — it's happening right here!

Vicky goes deep into the closet and wheels out a trolley bearing champagne, strawberries, sandwiches, napkins, glasses, etc. Pip gapes

Where did this come from?
Vicky Room service. I ordered champagne, smoked salmon sandwiches and wild strawberries. I said I was your secretary.
Pip You don't even look like a secretary.
Vicky That's what the waiter thought. He winked.
Pip Winked! Oh my God!
Vicky I had some champagne. I hope you don't mind.

Pip (*weakly*) No.
Vicky But before we eat — I'm going to run you a bath.
Pip A bath?

Vicky moves to a vase of flowers and selects some roses

Vicky Sprinkled with aromatic oils and rose petals. You smell of Brussels sprouts.
Pip Vicky, I should point out — I've never done this before.
Vicky You mean you're a virgin?
Pip No! I've never been unfaithful.
Vicky I should hope not. After all, you are a cabinet minister. There should be some standards.
Pip Oh, I've been tempted but I've always put my career first.
Vicky I notice you didn't say your marriage first.
Pip That goes without saying.
Vicky It never goes without saying. I thought you said she prefers her dogs to you?
Pip No, I didn't. (*Pause*) I said she prefers her horses to me. I'm not sure about the dogs.
Vicky Then why stay?
Pip Because of my career. It's important to me.
Vicky Then you're lucky to have met someone like me — totally reliable and utterly discreet.
Pip Discreet! You've got nothing on under your coat!
Vicky That's different. I felt like doing something romantic, daring and exciting. Don't you ever feel like that? Don't you ever follow your emotions?
Pip (*firmly*) No — I can't afford to.
Vicky Never mind — I've got enough emotion for both of us.

Vicky exits into the bathroom

The bathroom light comes on; we hear the sound of a bath being run

Pip makes sure the bathroom door is firmly closed. He chews thoughtfully on a sandwich and regards himself in the closet mirror

During the following, Higgs enters and stands silently behind Pip

Pip (*talking to his reflection*) Leave in the morning ... General hurly-burly ... Staff ... Cleaners ... Guests. Who'd know? As long as her buttons hold ... (*He sees Higgs' reflection and almost chokes*) Higgs! I thought you were going to knock?

Act I, Scene 1

Higgs I obtained a second key from reception. I thought it best.
Pip Well, knock in future.
Higgs Yes, sir. (*He spots the food*) You've got your appetite back then.
Pip Yes.
Higgs My word. Strawberries and champagne. This is nice. We normally get a flask and a few sandwiches. (*He takes a bite from a sandwich*)
Pip (*coldly*) It's not for you, Higgs.
Higgs (*mouthful*) What?
Pip It's for my secretary.
Higgs Oh. I've taken a bite.
Pip Then finish it.
Higgs (*swallowing*) Sorry, sir. (*He finishes the sandwich, looking hurt. He begins to ease off his shoes*)
Pip What are you doing?
Higgs Making myself comfortable.
Pip Well, don't. I don't think there's any immediate cause for concern — and I want an early night.
Higgs After you've dined with your secretary?
Pip Yes.
Higgs (*huffily*) Well, I didn't mean to intrude. I suppose I could use the chair on the landing. Not as comfortable but if that's the way things are …
Pip Stop looking like a spaniel who's been turned out of his favourite chair, Higgs. Can't you go to your room? I'll ring if I need you.
Higgs That may be too late — if this is a wet job.
Pip A wet job?
Higgs If you're to be terminated.
Pip Aren't you taking these letters a little too seriously?
Higgs It's not just the letters. You're being followed.
Pip Followed?
Higgs A stalker. Something Fielding reported last week. A woman was watching you from the Strangers' Gallery. He said that when you rose to speak she leaned forward and listened intently.
Pip A great many people listen to my speeches intently. They're not all like you, Higgs.
Higgs But he saw the woman again — following you in an old Mini as you strolled down Regent Street — the Mini was being driven at walking pace. She was also present when you were dining at the Mansion House. There's even a picture of her in one of the glossies. (*He moves to the desk and opens a magazine*) Here it is. Standing behind the Prime Minister's party. It gives everyone's name but hers.
Pip What does it say about her?
Higgs "Unidentified." Ever seen her before?
Pip No.
Higgs That surprises me. Fielding thought he saw you talking to her.

Pip I talk to a lot of people, Higgs. You can't expect me to remember them all.
Higgs No, I suppose not. But there's something else. We found a postcard on the pavement outside. Someone must have dropped it. It was a picture of the hotel. Your bedroom window was marked with a cross.
Pip My window? You're sure it wasn't the Prime Minister's window?
Higgs No.

They look at the french windows for a moment in silence

Your tap's running.
Pip I know.
Higgs Better switch it off. We don't want it dripping down on the Prime Minister... (*He moves to the bathroom door and puts his hand on the knob*)
Pip Higgs!

The sound of the running tap stops

Vicky emerges suddenly from the bathroom. She has a towel over her arm. She gives them a brisk smile

Higgs stands still, in stunned silence, through the following

Vicky Well, that's it, sir.
Pip (*blankly*) What?
Vicky I've turned the bed down — and opened the window. That's the trouble with these places — it's either roasting or as cold as charity. I mean it's not natural, is it?
Pip No.
Vicky And I'm sorry about the towel — it should have been replaced. I mean, you shouldn't have to make do with soiled linen — not a man of your stature. (*She moves around the room straightening things*) I blame those girls: they've only one thing on their minds — and you know what that is. (*She hands him a form from the desk*) Don't forget to mention it in your critique, sir. We won't know if you don't tell us. We should complain more often, that's what I say. Well, I'm going off now, sir. And I can only apologize once more for that ring round the bath. You don't want that — not a man of your calibre. (*She pauses by the door*) Will that be all, sir?
Pip (*emphatically*) Yes.

Vicky looks thoughtfully at the palm of her hand. Pip realizes incredulously that she's waiting for a tip. He tips her

Thank you. And I don't wish to be disturbed this evening.

Act I, Scene 1

Vicky takes the "Do not disturb" sign off the door knob and hands it to Pip

Vicky Then just hang this from your knob, sir. It says "Do not disturb" in three languages: English, French and German. Mind you, that does leave the rest of Europe — half the civilized world — and the sub-continents ... Apart from them you should get a peaceful night.

Vicky exits

Pip makes a great show of putting out the sign. Higgs breaks his stunned silence at last

Higgs Who was that?
Pip Obviously it was the maid.
Higgs She was wearing a raincoat.
Pip Well, she probably thinks it's going to rain. She was going off duty.
Higgs Ever seen her before?
Pip No. (*Anxiously*) Have you?
Higgs No — and I've got a memory for faces.
Pip Yes, of course. (*He closes up the magazine*)
Higgs I didn't see her come in.
Pip Well, never mind, she's gone now.
Higgs But what has she left behind? What did she have concealed under that coat?
Pip Nothing, Higgs.
Higgs Are you sure?
Pip What are you suggesting?
Higgs A trembler device.
Pip What?
Higgs And plastic explosive — now already placed in the bathroom. One false move, a little energetic scrubbing, and you could be completing your ablutions on the sea front.
Pip No, I think she was just the maid.
Higgs Better check ...

Higgs exits into the bathroom

Pip watches him anxiously from the door

Higgs returns, looking a shade uncertain

Higgs There are rose petals in the bath water.
Pip Yes.
Higgs (*after a pause*) Is that for medicinal purposes?

Pip Yes, I find it relaxing.
Higgs Really? I must remember to mention that to Mrs Higgs. She has difficulty relaxing.
Pip That doesn't surprise me, Higgs. Now, if you don't mind …
Higgs Perhaps if we brought up a sniffer dog …
Pip I don't want a sniffer dog. Good-night. (*He opens the outer door* L)
Higgs I'll check around.

Higgs exits

Pip (*closing the door and running a hand across his brow*) My God! I'm sweating. What an escape. What came over me? Twenty-five years of public service. Seven years getting adopted. Ten years on the back benches. Six years in the cabinet. Two years Deputy Leader. And I was prepared to throw it all away.

There is a discreet tapping on the door

(*Hissing through the door*) Can't you read? It says do not disturb. Go away.

There is the sound of George Reynold's voice, off

Pip sighs and opens the door

George Reynolds, the Home Secretary, enters. He is a few years older than Pip. He is silver-haired with a smooth, patrician manner which serves to hide a basic insecurity. During the following, he prowls the room peering into vases and behind picture frames

Sorry, George. I didn't realize it was you.
Reynolds (*sharply*) Who did you think it was?
Pip I thought it might be the press.
Reynolds What! I thought those jackals would be asleep by now. I can't afford to be seen here. I took a risk coming. (*He points significantly to the floor below*)
Pip I realize that.
Reynolds (*curiously*) You were expecting the press at this time of night?
Pip It was the meeting this evening. It aroused some interest.
Reynolds Yes — you certainly fell for that one. Bloody students. Have you seen them out there? They're foaming at the mouth. Has this room been checked?
Pip Yes.
Reynolds Good. (*He sees the refreshments for the first time*) Expecting someone, Pip?

Pip (*after a hesitation*) Yes — you, George.
Reynolds Champagne. Are we celebrating?
Pip We could be ...
Reynolds Then I'll come to the point. I won't use any names during this discussion but you'll know who I mean. What do you think of his performance over the last few weeks?
Pip He hasn't been at his best.
Reynolds He's going down like a pricked balloon.
Pip They say he's not well.
Reynolds He's a sick man.
Pip I've heard there's some trouble with the waterworks.
Reynolds Twenty-five minutes at the urinals this morning. I timed him. But it's not just the prostate — there's something else. They found him in his garden at the weekend — he'd collapsed. He'd been raking up a few leaves and even that was too much for him ...
Pip What was it?
Reynolds Heart.
Pip That's a surprise.
Reynolds (*nodding*) I didn't know he'd got one.
Pip (*smiling and then looking serious*) Still, I'm very sorry.
Reynolds Of course, we all are. But consider, he was clearing up a few leaves — suppose it had been a heavy fall of snow? We could have lost him ...
Pip That would have been a tragedy.
Reynolds Would it? I'm going to lower my voice now. (*He does*) He's becoming increasingly isolated and suspicious. His grip on the situation grows ever weaker. His speeches are poor and he's dividing the party. We're looking for leadership. We're looking to you. Will you stand against him?
Pip George, as you know, I've always been totally loyal to the Prime Minister.
Reynolds (*hissing*) It's no good me lowering my voice and avoiding his name if you're going to call him Prime Minister.
Pip Sorry, George.
Reynolds Your loyalty is beyond question. After all, you owe him your career. But the party may not wait for the inevitable. The question is this: if he is finished are you going to lie down with him like the faithful hound or are you going to lead the pack?
Pip I have given it some thought.
Reynolds Well, don't leave it too long. You've been an up and coming politician for some time. But many of us are that. Now is the time to be up and running.
Pip (*cautiously*) If the party feels that I can be of service, if my friends advise me ... Then, I would allow my name to go forward.
Reynolds You want it?

Pip (*promptly*) Yes.
Reynolds Then let's drink to it.

Pip fills Reynolds' glass

There is knocking at the door: two short, two long

Reynolds (*startled*) Who's that?

Pip listens and then smiles

Pip It's all right, George. Two short — two long. That's security. They're very attentive tonight. (*He listens to the following with his hand on the door*)
Reynolds Good. You should take care. We need you. You're everyone's choice. Your career has been impeccable. A model of discreet advancement. All the others are open to question. Shadowy pasts — dirty dealings. But not you, Pip — that's your strength ...
Pip Thank you, George. (*He opens the door*)

Vicky breezes in

Vicky (*brightly*) I'm back.

Reynolds stares at Vicky in surprise. Pip stares at Reynolds, horrifed. Vicky follows Pip's stare

Reynolds (*rising*) And who is this, Pip?
Vicky Daphne Smart. Woman's Own Christian Family Journal.
Reynolds Woman's Own ?
Vicky Christian Family Journal. I was here earlier.
Pip (*quickly*) Yes, she was here earlier.
Reynolds You're giving an interview?
Pip Yes.
Reynolds Isn't it rather late?
Vicky Mr Conway was busy — he said I could come back later. Ah, there's my pad. I knew I'd left it somewhere ... (*She crosses to the desk, picks up the pad and pen and sits, pen poised expectantly*)
Pip Well, it is a little late and I think I said all I intended to say, Miss —— ?
Vicky Smart. Just a few more questions, Mr Conway. We were talking about your marriage ...
Pip Were we?
Vicky You've been married over twenty years, I believe ——
Pip Yes.

Act I, Scene 1   17

Vicky Wonderful. The Woman's Own Christian Family Circle are very concerned with family values.
Reynolds I thought you said Journal?
Vicky We merged. My — isn't it warm in here? (*She loosens her coat*)

Pip looks tense

Reynolds Let me take your coat, Miss Smart.

Reynolds assists Vicky off with her coat. Pip turns away with a faint groan. Vicky emerges from her coat. She is wearing a short dress. Pip turns and stares

    (*Regarding him curiously*) Is something the matter, Pip?
Pip No.
Vicky Over twenty years. Splendid. Do you ever quarrel?
Pip Not really.
Vicky And you've never found your marriage restrictive — even a little boring?
Pip No.
Vicky Then it's still a love affair?
Pip I suppose so.
Vicky May I say — "passionate love affair"?

Pip glances at Reynolds who smiles encouragingly

Pip If you wish.
Vicky (*slowly*) How many times do you ——?
Pip (*alarmed*) What?
Vicky — tell your wife that you love her? Is it on a daily basis?
Pip Well, I am away a great deal.
Vicky I suppose that's why you're so passionate. What is it about your wife that still fascinates, still captivates you after all these years?
Pip I don't know ... I ...
Vicky She's a horsewoman I believe?
Pip Yes.
Vicky Do you find that attractive — a woman astride a huge stallion, grasping his broad girth between her thighs, bending the proud beast to her will? Do you find that stimulating in a woman?
Pip I haven't really thought about it.
Vicky Doesn't your wife hunt?
Reynolds (*quickly*) Mr Conway doesn't hunt and has no strong views on blood sports.
Pip Quite.

Vicky No, but it is my experience that the hunting fraternity can be rather — (*she pauses*) ruttish.
Pip (*staring*) Ruttish?
Vicky But perhaps you find that aspect of your wife exciting. After a long day in the saddle, all that leaping and galloping and gripping, coupled with the excitement of the kill, the scent of blood in her nostrils, splattered in mud, and that ruttish look in her eye — you at her feet, removing her boots. Do you find that exciting?

Pip and Reynolds stare at Vicky in stunned silence. Reynolds clears his throat

Reynolds Well, I must go, Pip. I have things to do — and I'm sure you have ... (*He stares at Vicky in wonder*) Good-night, Miss Smart.
Vicky (*sweetly*) Good-night.

Reynolds exits

Pip sees Reynolds out and then turns accusingly to Vicky

Pip You said you had nothing on under your coat.
Vicky Disappointed?
Pip Why did you say that?
Vicky I thought you might find it tempting.
Pip I did. But not now. You must go.
Vicky You're becoming monotonous. (*She moves to the door and secures the safety chain*)
Pip What are you doing?
Vicky Come here. (*She moves to the french windows, opens the curtains wide and looks out*) Look out of the window.
Pip (*suspiciously*) The window?

Vicky takes Pip's hand and draws him towards her

Vicky Look at that vast sea — that infinite sky. Doesn't it make you feel small and insignificant?
Pip No. I'm a cabinet minister.
Vicky But doesn't it make you feel that nothing really matters but we two? That we should live for the moment. Suppose the world was to end tonight, Pip?
Pip (*sharply*) Why should it?
Vicky Well, it will for someone — it does every night.
Pip Yes, but why me? What made you say that? Why did you come here?
Vicky Isn't that obvious? (*She puts her arms around him*)

Act I, Scene 2   19

There is the loud report of a firework from outside

Pip starts but Vicky holds him close, turning him with his back to the french windows

Pip What was that?
Vicky (*softly*) Just a big bang ... How very appropriate ...

They kiss slowly. Pip realizes he's been turned so that he has his back to the french windows; he slowly circles Vicky round so that the position is reversed

The Lights fade

A rocket erupts against the night sky

CURTAIN

SCENE 2

The same. An hour later

When the CURTAIN *rises the lounge is illuminated by a table lamp. The bedroom is in darkness except for a shaft of light from the open door of the bathroom which reveals the shadowy figure of Vicky in bed*

Vicky's clothes from SCENE 1 *are scattered around the lounge*

There is an insistent tapping on the outer door of the suite; this continues throughout the following

Pip enters the lounge from the bathroom, tucking in his shirt and slipping on his shoes

Pip I'm coming. I'm coming. (*He switches on the main light. He sees Vicky's clothes strewn around the room and bundles them into the closet. He smooths down his hair*) One moment! (*He checks that the bathroom and bedroom doors are firmly closed then crosses and unchains the door*)

Reynolds enters the lounge

George! Couldn't this have waited until the morning? It's late.
Reynolds We have to move quickly, Pip. The PM's thinking of another reshuffle.

Pip Another one! Who told you?
Reynolds Coupland. I met him in the bar.
Pip How does he know?
Reynolds He seems to know everything. You may have to make an open challenge.
Pip Open? I don't know about open, George. The PM's fading fast. Shouldn't we wait until he's faded a little more?
Reynolds Pip — he wants to bring in fresh blood.
Pip What?
Reynolds Coupland says he's tired of shuffling the same greasy pack!
Pip Greasy pack!
Reynolds Just a figure of speech. I don't suppose he meant you personally.
Pip Don't you? It's all right for you, George. You haven't been shuffled as often as I have. I'm greasier than most.
Reynolds There's something else. Coupland thinks the PM may wish to nominate his successor.
Pip He may nominate me.
Reynolds He may. But I don't think it's likely. Neither does Coupland.
Pip (*alarmed*) You didn't discuss this with Coupland? I thought you were going to be discreet?
Reynolds I was discreet.
Pip (*dryly*) Did you lower your voice?
Reynolds I merely floated the idea of a successor. I mentioned the prostate, the angina, and then you.
Pip So I come after the prostate and the angina! I sound like a disease.
Reynolds That's what Coupland thought. He laughed.
Pip Why did he laugh?
Reynolds He said if the Prime Minister had the choice between the angina and you — he'd choose the angina.
Pip (*frowning*) You're forgetting — I am his deputy, George.
Reynolds I pointed that out to Coupland. He said he thought the PM had appointed you on the principle that the party may not like him but look at the alternative.
Pip I knew Coupland didn't like me. I wish you hadn't brought him into this.
Reynolds I don't know what he's got against you. He simply says there's something about you that doesn't ring true …
Pip (*anxiously*) Did he say what it was?
Reynolds No. It may be that he's merely representing the views of his employer. They don't like your stance on media ownership, Pip.
Pip Don't they? Well, hard luck. They don't run the country yet, George.
Reynolds Not quite. But it doesn't do to offend them. The press only have to find a weakness and they can destroy you.
Pip (*blanching*) What weakness?

Act I, Scene 2

Reynolds What's the matter, Pip? You look agitated.
Pip (*after a hesitation*) I'm suddenly aware of the awesome task before me, George.
Reynolds It's a task that can be shared ... You'll need a running mate.
Pip Well, I had thought of you, George.
Reynolds No, I seek nothing for myself. Well, possibly the Foreign Office — but that would come later. At the moment I prefer to remain in the shadows.
Pip Then who?
Reynolds I'm going to say something that may surprise you. I'm going to say — Berryman.
Pip (*exploding*) Berryman!
Reynolds I knew that would surprise you.
Pip It does. He's only got one eye.
Reynolds I don't think we should hold that against him. In the land of the blind the one-eyed man is king. And he is on the front bench.
Pip Only just — he's almost out the door. And he's without a portfolio.
Reynolds Precisely. The Prime Minister took it from him and Berryman has never forgiven him. That makes him a willing ally. He was at the peak of his career and Henderson destroyed him.
Pip Yes, and he's been as pissed as a frog ever since. He's unreliable on industrial relations, he's unreliable on immigration, he's unreliable on law and order — and he's particularly unreliable when he's got six malts inside him.
Reynolds But he has charisma.
Pip Haven't I got charisma?
Reynolds (*looking at Pip doubtfully*) With all due respect, Pip, a pair of brightly-coloured braces does not necessarily indicate charisma. You're considered a safe pair of hands but Berryman has glamour. The party workers love him; he's adored in the shires. And don't forget where he lost that eye — the Falklands. He has a fine military record — and nothing enhances a politician's reputation more than a brush with death. And he can bring you a hundred back-benchers ...
Pip (*after a hesitation*) Are you sure about this, George?
Reynolds Don't underestimate him, Pip. When I saw him a few days ago he'd been drinking heavily but when I hinted what we had in mind ——
Pip You've already discussed this with him!
Reynolds I was discreet. But once he'd got my drift a look of deep cunning came into his eye.
Pip Which one?
Reynolds It was like looking down the barrel of a loaded gun.
Pip But he wears an eye patch. He runs around the back benches like someone out of *Treasure Island*.

Reynolds He can deliver the right wing of the party, Pip. At least meet him — talk to him. You can always get rid of him later.
Pip Well, if you think I should ...
Reynolds I'll arrange a meeting. Time is of the essence ... (*He moves to the door* L)

Vicky stirs sleepily, fumbles for the light and accidentally switches on the radio

(*Stopping and staring*) That's your radio.
Pip Yes.
Reynolds I didn't hear it before.
Pip Must have been a power surge ...

Vicky fiddles desperately with the radio switches, increasing the volume and changing stations, and switches lamps on and off

Excuse me.

Pip moves into the bedroom, closing the door firmly behind him

Reynolds approaches the door and listens curiously. Pip and Vicky engage in dumb show. Pip finally succeeds in switching off the radio. Vicky switches on the bedside lamps Reynolds reaches for the door handle

Higgs enters the lounge silently

Higgs sees Reynolds. He creeps up behind him and seizes him in an arm lock, forcing him to the ground. Reynolds shrieks with pain

Pip emerges hurriedly from the bedroom, closing the door behind him

Pip Higgs!
Higgs (*calmly*) Don't worry, sir. I've got him. No need for alarm. Ever seen him before?
Pip Yes — he's the Home Secretary.
Higgs Oh. Sorry, sir ...

Pip and Higgs assist Reynolds to his feet

I do apologize — only we're on red alert this evening ...
Pip Would you wait outside, Higgs?
Higgs Sir.

Higgs exits

Pip Sorry about that, George.
Reynolds He almost took my arm off!
Pip He's a little over-protective.
Reynolds He's a gorilla. He should be in a cage. I have no feeling in this hand.
Pip I think that's what they call minimum force.
Reynolds Minimum force! That was police brutality. And I have to get up and defend them in the House! I need a drink of water.

Reynolds exits into the bathroom

Pip waits anxiously

Reynolds returns with a glass of water

Reynolds (*regarding Pip curiously*) There are rose petals in the bath water ...
Pip Yes.
Reynolds And what's that aroma ...?
Pip Oils and spices. (*Pause*) I find them very relaxing ...
Reynolds Do you? (*Pause. Casually*) Been missing Bunty this week, Pip?
Pip Rather. I wish she was here.
Reynolds Good. Because I took the liberty of ringing her earlier today.
Pip You rang Bunty?
Reynolds Yes — I advised her to come down.
Pip (*appalled*) What did she say?
Reynolds Well, she was going hunting but she said she'd catch the overnight train.
Pip Overnight train! What time? When will it get in? How long have I got?
Reynolds (*staring*) I'm not sure. Is there a problem?
Pip No, but I have a great deal to get through. I have to work on my speech ...
Reynolds She'll understand. After all, she's the granddaughter of a prime minister, Pip. And it's important that she's here to meet the press tomorrow. We need a picture of you both holding hands and looking into the future. Your idyllic marriage is one of our strengths. It's worth a million votes. Pity there aren't any children but we can't have everything — we'll have to make do with the labradors. Has she recovered from her fall?
Pip Which one?
Reynolds Has she had another one?
Pip Yes, but not as bad as the first one. Hasn't got over that yet. Still a little dazed — can't focus. Came round in Harrods last week clutching a jar of pickle — didn't know how she got there.

Reynolds Perhaps she should give up riding for a while. She's important to us. And she's better-looking than Henderson's wife — she's as ugly as a wart.
Pip You make it sound like a beauty contest, George.
Reynolds It is, Pip. So look your best tomorrow. You seem a little jaded. You haven't been overdoing it?
Pip No.
Reynolds Good. (*He moves to the door*)
Pip George, don't you think I have charisma?
George Of course you do. (*Pause*) Wear your colourful braces tomorrow.

Reynolds exits

Pip pours himself a drink

Vicky enters from the bedroom. She is wearing one of Pip's shirts

Vicky Has he gone?
Pip Yes. And so must you. Things are moving faster than I thought. (*He moves to the closet*) You must leave at once.
Vicky Why?
Pip (*turning incredulously*) Why? Because Reynolds is already suspicious. The Prime Minister's in the room below — and that bed creaks. Also my wife's on the overnight train and I don't know when she'll arrive. Then there's my secretary; the bonfire's made her restless. And don't forget Higgs — there's always Higgs.
Vicky (*coldly*) What are you trying to say, Pip — that it's not convenient?
Pip Of course it's not convenient!
Vicky Then why don't you drop me down the laundry chute? Isn't that what you do with something soiled and discarded?
Pip (*hurriedly*) You're not soiled and discarded. You're the best thing that's ever happened to me.
Vicky You're gabbling, it doesn't sound convincing.
Pip Of course I'm gabbling. I'm on a tight schedule. You must go.
Vicky Now you're repeating yourself.
Pip I can't endanger my marriage.
Vicky You mean your idyllic marriage?
Pip You were listening.
Vicky I didn't have to listen. I've seen the pictures. You and your wife leaning over a five-bar gate. The labradors leaping around you. You with your arm around her waist while she looks faintly pickled.
Pip She wasn't pickled.
Vicky She looked in a state of shock.

Act I, Scene 2   25

Pip That was because of her fall.
Vicky I thought it may have been the surprise at finding your arm round her waist. You were very convincing. I must say, as one actor to another, you've certainly got a line through that character.
Pip I don't act.
Vicky (*after a pause*) So you meant it when you said I was the best thing that ever happened to you?
Pip Yes.

Vicky puts her arms around Pip. They move into a kiss

Higgs enters and coughs discreetly

Pip and Vicky break apart

Vicky darts into the bathroom

Pip and Higgs regard each other

Pip (*cautiously*) Higgs, have you met my wife ...?
Higgs Yes — on several occasions.
Pip That wasn't my wife.
Higgs I know.
Pip I suppose you're shocked.
Higgs No, nothing shocks me any more. Not after my years on the Force. I've seen more life than a tramp's vest.

Higgs helps himself to a sandwich. Pip notes this but doesn't respond

> Do you know, when we had that bomb scare on Monday night there were six hundred guests shivering in that car park and we only had four hundred and fifty registered. That's what makes security so difficult. (*He pours himself a drink*) Of course I recognized her.

Pip You did?
Higgs I never forget a face. It took some time but it's come back to me. She's the maid.
Pip (*relieved*) Yes.
Higgs In here a little while ago with that implausible story about the towels. I must say I thought you could have done better but there you are. Not that I don't understand. (*He makes himself comfortable and takes another sandwich*)
Pip Do you mind if I join you, Higgs?
Higgs (*failing to spot the irony*) Please do.

Pip sits down

Do you know the most alluring thing about a woman?
Pip (*distractedly*) I'm not sure ... Beauty?
Higgs No.
Pip Sensitivity?
Higgs No.
Pip Personality?
Higgs No.
Pip Then what is it?
Higgs Availability. And my God — she's available — I can see that.
Pip No — it wasn't like that, Higgs.
Higgs Then how do you explain it? A casual stranger who came in to turn down the covers and leave a mint. (*He leans forward suggestively*) What happened? Was she bending over the bed? Did her skirt tighten? Was there a sudden moment of lust? And was she drawn to you as all women are to men of power? What was she like on a scale of one to ten?
Pip (*desperately*) Higgs, she is not the maid!
Higgs What?
Pip She's the girl from the Mansion House. She won't leave. She's in the bathroom in my shirt and her clothes are in the closet.
Higgs (*staring*) From the Mansion House?
Pip (*seizing the magazine*) Her picture is in the magazine. You looked at it. It's one of those faces you never forget, Higgs! (*He thrusts the picture in front of Higgs*)
Higgs (*studying the photo*) My God! This puts a different complexion on things. She could be a swallow.
Pip A swallow?
Higgs I never thought of that.
Pip What's a swallow?
Higgs Special Branch parlance for an agent of a foreign power who exchanges sexual favours for state secrets.
Pip Higgs, I don't know any state secrets. No-one tells me anything. I haven't any secrets.
Higgs (*after a pause*) You have now — a big one. Her. This could be blackmail. She'd better not leave until I've checked her out. You say her clothes are in the closet ...?

Higgs goes into the closet. He re-emerges stuffing Vicky's clothes into a holdall

Pip What are you doing?
Higgs I'm taking these to my room. Go through the pockets — search the linings ...
Pip What for?

Act I, Scene 2   27

Higgs Recordings, micro-films — who knows? (*Pause*) There weren't any flashing lights during this experience — I mean more than usual …?
Pip I don't remember.
Higgs (*lewdly*) She made you forget everything, did she?
Pip Don't start that again, Higgs.
Higgs (*shrugging*) If you want to be prudish … (*He takes another sandwich*) Keep her here until I get back.
Pip That shouldn't be difficult, Higgs. I can't get rid of her.

Higgs exits

Pip hesitates in front of the closet. He opens the door and looks inside. He comes out with Vicky's handbag. He glances at the bathroom door. He begins to open the bag

There is a tap on the outer door

Pip throws the bag back into the closet and closes the door. He opens the outer door

Lorna enters

Pip Lorna! It's terribly late.
Lorna I just wondered what you thought of it.
Pip What?
Lorna The speech.
Pip I haven't read it yet.
Lorna (*surprised*) But you usually read it straight away.
Pip I've been busy. I'll read it now. (*He picks up the speech, then hesitates*) I thought you didn't like to be here while I read it?
Lorna Tonight's different.
Pip (*wearily*) Yes.
Lorna I think I've made a few improvements.
Pip I can see that. (*He reads through the speech at high speed*) Good. Very good. What an opening. Telling phrase. Very apt. Good point. Interesting comparison. Funny line. Nice conclusion. Wraps everything up. I like it.

Lorna stares at him in astonishment

Lorna Are you in a hurry?
Pip No. (*He leans back languidly in his chair*)

Lorna picks up a napkin

What are you doing?

Lorna I was going to eat.
Pip I'll have something sent to your room.
Lorna Isn't there enough here?
Pip No. I'm hungry. (*Referring to a page under the speech*) What are these notes?
Lorna They're for your interview with Coupland. (*She reaches for a crisp*)

Pip frowns

Lorna withdraws her hand

I'm concerned about your television manner.
Pip What's wrong with it?
Lorna You use the interviewer's first name too much — it sounds ingratiating. And you're always saying, "I'm glad you asked me that"; it gets repetitive — especially when you don't answer the question. And don't say, "I mean", and, "You know", quite so much. We assume you mean what you say and how can we know until you tell us? (*She picks up a sandwich*)

Pip glares at Lorna over the notes. She returns the sandwich to the plate

Pip What's this about my lip?
Lorna You bite your lower lip when you're in a corner — it makes you look furtive. Don't do it.
Pip I don't do it. (*He bites his lower lip*)
Lorna You do. (*She smiles*) That's funny — you're doing it now. And don't let them put too much make-up on you. You tend to look embalmed — your face looks orange and your eyes are like currants.
Pip Currants! You're not doing much for my confidence. I must look like a gingerbread man! And put that champagne down!
Lorna (*staring*) Pip, there's champagne in this glass — you have yours. If it's not for me, whose is it?
Pip (*after a hesitation*) Reynolds was here. He wants me to run with Berryman.
Lorna Berryman!
Pip He can deliver the right wing of the party.
Lorna You don't need the right wing. You have the centre and the left — that's all you need.
Pip I need all the support I can get. Reynolds says he has charisma.
Lorna He also has a glass eye.
Pip I don't think we should hold that against him.
Lorna He's been known to drop it into people's wine glasses. And he drinks.

Act I, Scene 2

Pip No-one's perfect.
Lorna And Reynolds suggested him?
Pip Yes.
Lorna Don't you think that's strange? Reynolds can't stand him.
Pip Our personal feelings don't come into this, Lorna. And Reynolds is very astute.
Lorna Well, I think it's mad. But I'm sure you'd sooner listen to Reynolds. After all, he's a man. (*She moves to the french windows*)
Pip (*following Lorna cautiously*) Lorna, you know I always listen to you. But I have to act quickly. The Prime Minister is fading ...
Lorna Are you sure?
Pip Reynolds says he could go any time.

Lorna sighs

What's the matter?
Lorna We both seem to be waiting for people to die. The Prime Minister. Bunty.
Pip Don't say that.
Lorna I went for a walk on the beach. That damned bonfire was still blazing. The more I stared into those flames the more feverish I became. I felt consumed ... You know what I mean, Pip.
Pip (*uneasily*) I think so.
Lorna I felt aroused.
Pip (*babbling*) Ah. That's the bonfire. It has that effect on some people — arsonists for example; they get terribly excited — something to do with the flames ——
Lorna (*sharply*) I wasn't asking for an explanation. I thought why have I waited all these years? Why have you waited, Pip?
Pip Because of Bunty.
Lorna Are you sure there is not another reason? Isn't it because of your career? That you don't trust me. That you're afraid to put yourself in my hands for fear that I might use it against you later?
Pip Of course not. I trust you.
Lorna Then why wait? Who'd ever know? (*She kisses Pip fiercely*)

Pip looks nervously towards the bathroom

Pip We'd know, Lorna. We must behave honourably. But one day ...
Lorna One day! Pip, they say you're a promising politician — well, just for once, stop promising and bloody perform!
Pip Lorna, Bunty's on the night train.
Lorna She won't be here until morning. Do you know what I have under this dress?

Pip (*groaning*) Oh, God! No.
Lorna Some incredibly sexy underwear. Would you like to see it?
Pip No! Higgs will be back in a minute. You must go.
Lorna (*moving to the desk and turning*) Then kiss me.

Pip kisses Lorna. She holds him in a tight embrace. As she does so she picks up his room key and slips it in her pocket. He guides her to the door, his arm still about her

Pip Now you really must leave. I've a great deal to get through before morning. But don't think this is easy …

Pip opens the door, kisses Lorna again and says a silent good-night to her with a despairing gesture

Lorna exits

Pip closes the door

Vicky emerges from the bathroom

Pip turns and sees Vicky

Vicky Who was that?
Pip Miss Fiske — my secretary.
Vicky She was here earlier.
Pip Yes.
Vicky What's she like?
Pip Very ordinary — glasses.
Vicky What was that popping sound?
Pip What popping sound?
Vicky After she said, "Who'd ever know?" there was popping sound — like someone pulling a cork. What was that?
Pip I've no idea.
Vicky Then there was another popping sound.
Pip Would you stop talking about popping sounds?
Vicky That was when she was leaving. Only this time it sounded more like someone clearing a blocked drain. (*Pause*) You were kissing her, weren't you?
Pip (*after a hesitation*) Well, we have a close working relationship — and in moments of triumph — achievement — great emotional moments — we have been known to — kiss.
Vicky (*studying Pip*) Don't you take a long time to say something? I suppose

that's because you're a politician. And did you have a great emotional moment tonight?
Pip You could say that.
Vicky Are you going to be Prime Minister?
Pip (*concerned*) How much did you hear in there?
Vicky I've never slept with a Prime Minister before. It's a first.
Pip I'm not Prime Minister yet — and I won't be if you don't get out of here.
Vicky (*opening the closet door*) Where are my clothes?
Pip Higgs has taken them.
Vicky They won't suit him.
Pip He wanted to check them out.
Vicky Why?
Pip He thinks you may be a spy.
Vicky Do you think I'm a spy?
Pip No. (*Pause*) Are you?
Vicky No, I'm just a woman in love. A little wan — sighing — sniffing at flowers — crying for no good reason — a little dreamy. And now I find the green shoots of my affection have been trampled on.
Pip Trampled on?
Vicky You've been unfaithful to me — and so soon.
Pip Vicky, how could I have been unfaithful to you? I didn't even know you when Lorna and I became close ——
Vicky You should have waited. I was bound to happen, you know that. I was your destiny.
Pip (*shaking his head*) Destiny.

Vicky heads for the bedroom

Where are you going?
Vicky Well, since you've got my clothes — I'm going back to bed.

Vicky goes into the bedroom and climbs between the sheets

There is a knock on the outer door. Pip ensures the bedroom door is firmly closed and moves to the outer door

Pip Higgs? (*He opens the outer door*)

Lionel Berryman enters. He is a tall, imposing man in his fifties. He is wearing a velvet eye patch. He has the dignified bearing of a man who's excessively drunk. He has a smoking cigar in one hand and a firework in the other

Pip Lionel.

Berryman Hallo, Pip. (*He advances* C)
Pip (*following anxiously*) What's that in your hand, Lionel?
Berryman A cigar.
Pip No, in the other hand.
Berryman Oh, this — a firework. Took them off a student — emptied the greasy toad's pockets. Want one?
Pip No, thank you.

Berryman lights the firework from his cigar. He opens the french windows and throws out the cigar. He turns with the firework still in his hand

Berryman That'll teach the buggers to throw fireworks.
Pip Lionel, you threw the cigar.
Berryman What?
Pip The firework's still in your hand.
Berryman Oh. So it is. (*He returns to the french windows and throws out the firework*)

Immediately there is a loud bang, off

That was close. Reminds me of the time the pin came out of a grenade at Goose Green. You're sure you don't want to throw one?
Pip Quite. (*He closes the curtains*) Lionel, you are aware that this meeting is supposed to be confidential.
Berryman Absolutely. (*He crosses, sits and lights another cigar*)
Pip And it is rather late.
Berryman I was detained in the bar. Tradesmen mainly but decent types. They were all a bit nervous with those students and anarchists foaming at the mouth but I calmed them down. I said what have those buggers ever done for the country? They've never been under fire — they've never known shot and shell. What do they know about sacrifice? Then do you know what I did?
Pip I think I can guess.
Berryman I took out the eye and passed it along the bar. It went from hand to hand. I said that's what I call sacrifice. You could have heard a pin drop ... Well, someone threw up but you always get the odd squeamish type. That reminds me — did the buggers give me it back? People are so light-fingered these days. (*He raises his eye patch*)
Pip It's still there, Lionel.
Berryman It's a new one — what do you think?
Pip It's very good.
Berryman Think they've got the colour right ... Sort of hazel?
Pip It's perfect.

Act I, Scene 2

Berryman It moves.
Pip It doesn't.
Berryman Amazing what they can do these days. I know a poor blighter in the Oman, had to make do with a marble.
Pip I certainly don't think you need the eye patch.
Berryman Oh. I thought it made me look more rakish.
Pip That's the problem, Lionel — you can look too rakish. I think you look more intelligent without it.
Berryman (*flattered*) Oh. Well, if you think so ... (*He removes the eye patch*)
Pip (*after a pause*) So quite a few people know you're here, Lionel.
Berryman Well, you couldn't expect me to pass through the lobby unnoticed, Pip. (*He indicates the champagne*) What's this?
Pip Champagne.
Berryman No — won't do at all. Need something to settle the stomach. It's like a flock of pigeons down here. (*He stands up, discarding his cigar*)
Pip (*anxiously*) You're not going to be sick, are you, Lionel?
Berryman (*looking around*) They usually have a sort of fridge — full of miniatures — stock it every day ... (*He opens the closet door*) Ah, here it is.
Pip No, that's the trouser press, Lionel. The drinks cabinet is over there.
Berryman Oh yes ... (*He struggles with the cabinet*)
Pip The door's at the front, Lionel.
Berryman Got it. (*He takes a miniature whisky out of the cabinet, pauses by the open door of the closet and studies himself in the mirror*) Is that me?
Pip Yes.
Berryman You're right — I do look more intelligent. And calm. You wouldn't believe what's going on inside, Pip.
Pip I think I could.
Berryman No, I was referring to my emotions. I had the same feeling when I went into action: excitement mingled with fear — and a sense of exultation. (*He returns to the sofa*) So you think our time has come?
Pip Everything points to it.
Berryman He doesn't suspect?
Pip No, he trusts me — as much as he trusts anyone.
Berryman Don't be too sure about that. I thought he trusted me once. Be careful, Pip.
Pip Lionel, I think I should tell you that the PM has a serious heart condition. He may not be in a position to influence events.
Berryman (*surprised*) Heart condition. Who told you that?
Pip George Reynolds.
Berryman Do you trust Reynolds?
Pip Yes. Don't you?

Berryman No. Had to thrash him at Eton. He never forgave me.
Pip He's right behind us, Lionel.
Berryman That's the last place I'd want him to be.
Pip But it was George who recommended you. He was here this evening for that very purpose.
Berryman Was he?
Pip So you see he doesn't bear malice.

During the following speech, Pip makes anxious silencing gestures, downward motions with the palms of his hands

Berryman Don't flatter him, Pip. If he doesn't seek revenge it's not because he hasn't the malice — it's because he hasn't the spirit. And I still find it strange that he recommended me. He avoided me the last time. They all did. I was like a great tree ready to fall — and they were all fearful of being crushed under its weight. Well, now it's Henderson's turn. He's going to know what it's like — having greatness snatched from you ... (*He rises again and begins to breath deeply through his nose*) Must have some fresh air ... (*He moves towards the french windows*)
Pip You are going to be sick. (*He snatches his bowler from the closet and follows Berryman*)

Berryman opens the french windows and breathes in deeply

Berryman That's better.
Pip I'd come away from the window, Lionel.
Berryman Why?
Pip Death threats. My bodyguard thinks they may shoot me through the window.

Pip closes the french windows and draws the curtains

Berryman Who are they?
Pip We don't know.
Berryman (*sadly*) No-one wants to kill me any more, Pip. There was a time when they all wanted to have a shot at me. The Red Brigade, the Angry Brigade, the IRA, the PLO, Red Dawn, Shining Light, Animal Lib. Even the Ratepayers' Association. And when it was at its height — do you know what the bugger did? He took my bodyguards away. He said that I didn't need them — that it was a needless expense. He was hoping someone would top me!

Pip returns to making silencing gestures

Act I, Scene 2

Why do you keep doing that?
Pip The Prime Minister's in the room below.
Berryman Oh. Then you're right to be cautious. He may be an old man but he has the hearing of a shit-house rat. And if he knew you were talking to me — he'd reduce you to a footnote. (*Pause*) Heart, did you say?
Pip Yes.
Berryman Tricky things — hearts ... Only have to stop for a few seconds, I believe.
Pip Yes.
Berryman Any sudden shock.
Pip Indeed.
Berryman Think of it. We could be a heartbeat away from success.
Pip I have thought about it.
Berryman I consulted my doctor last week. I'm in fine shape, Pip.
Pip Good.
Berryman And I'm ready to lead you.
Pip (*staring*) Lead us? Lionel, I think there's been some misunderstanding.
Berryman Misunderstanding?
Pip We don't actually see you as Prime Minister.
Berryman You don't?
Pip Didn't George Reynolds make that clear?
Berryman No.
Pip That's odd. No — we see you as the Deputy Prime Minister.
Berryman But that's your job.
Pip No — I shall be Prime Minister.
Berryman (*incredulously*) You?
Pip Yes. Why not?
Berryman Well, I'm not denying that you're an up and coming politician. But are you ready?
Pip I think so.
Berryman No, if you were ready you'd have said "Yes" — not "I think so". You have promise, Pip, but you're not ready — not yet. But you will be. I am on record as saying I see you as the next Prime Minister — but one.
Pip And I suppose you're the one?
Berryman I have this feeling, Pip.
Pip (*sighing*) Is it destiny?
Berryman Yes, that's it — destiny. I feel it very strongly tonight.
Pip Didn't you feel it very strongly the last time, Lionel?
Berryman Not like this. You don't feel it, do you? You lack something. You're too soft. You're like a cushion — you take on the shape of the last person who sat on you. You're not ruthless enough.
Pip I'm learning, Lionel, and let me be ruthless enough to tell you that a number of my supporters feel you shouldn't even be Deputy Prime Minister.

Berryman (*staring*) Why not?
Pip They're concerned about the drinking, Lionel ...
Berryman Drinking? What drinking?
Pip Your drinking.
Berryman Oh, that. Well, I have had a problem, I agree. But I've got it under control — virtually cured.
Pip (*drily*) Congratulations.
Berryman Thank you.
Pip But the party feels ...
Berryman Oh, what does the party feel?
Pip That they need a safe pair of hands. Now, we don't need your support, Lionel — we can do without it. But for the sake of party unity — I'd like you to join us.
Berryman And suppose I say no?
Pip Then I'm afraid as far as you're concerned, it's political oblivion. Is that ruthless enough for you?
Berryman I see ...
Pip Of course I'll quite understand if you feel you can't come with us.
Berryman (*after a hesitation*) I didn't say that. (*He rises from the sofa*) "What you have said I will consider. What you have to say I will with patience hear, and in time meet and discuss such high things." Now I must rest — I'm pissed. (*He staggers into the bedroom, falls down on the bed beside Vicky and falls asleep*)
Pip Lionel!

Pip follows Berryman into the bedroom

Vicky sits up and puts on a lamp. Pip and Vicky engage in dumb show

> *The outer door opens and Lorna enters. She looks around the deserted lounge and smiles. She exits into the bathroom undoing the buttons on her shirt*

Pip and Vicky hear the bathroom door close. Pip holds a finger to his lips. Vicky switches off the lamp and ducks under the blankets. Pip returns to the lounge. He looks curiously round the room

> *Lorna enters the bedroom from the bathroom clad in her underwear*

Lorna sees the shadowy figure of Berryman on the bed. She cuddles up beside him

There's a tapping on the outer door. Pip opens it

Act I, Scene 2

Henderson, the Prime Minister, enters. He is a small man in his sixties with sharp, darting eyes and a watchful manner

Henderson I know it's late — I hope I'm not disturbing you, Philip.

Lorna stops caressing Berryman and switches on the light. Vicky sits up. Berryman sits up. He stares from one woman to the other and falls back. Vicky and Lorna continue to regard each other

Pip moves to the bedroom door. He looks in and casually closes the door

Pip Not at all, Prime Minister ...

The Lights fade

CURTAIN

ACT II

Scene 1

The same. A few minutes later

In the lounge, Henderson is sitting on the sofa with his back to the room and Pip is fiddling with the sandwiches, trying to find a fresh one. In the unlit bedroom, Berryman is still lying prostrate on the bed and Vicky is crouched in the shadows. There is no sign of Lorna

Pip Would you care for a sandwich, Prime Minister?
Henderson Hm. Smoked salmon, strawberries, champagne. Quite a feast.
Pip I'm afraid the champagne's rather flat.
Henderson (*taking a sandwich*) Yes — and this sandwich is a little curly around the edges. (*With a sly smile*) Something you prepared earlier, Philip?
Pip I thought you'd call — but not quite this late.
Henderson Perhaps you didn't expect a man of my years to be out at this time?
Pip (*with a forced laugh*) A man of your years? You'll see us all out, Prime Minister.
Henderson (*quietly*) I intend to.
Pip What?
Henderson Churchill was my age when he shouldered the responsibilities of war. He took on a fifty year old and won.
Pip Right. (*Pause*) Is the champagne a good idea? I could send down for some cocoa.
Henderson (*frowning*) I don't need cocoa. There's nothing wrong with my digestion.
Pip Splendid. As I've always said: you're as tough as old boots, John.
Henderson Old boots? Well, I don't exactly warm to the image, Philip, but I approve of the sentiment. So you don't think I'm quite ready for the sunny uplands of retirement?

Pip gives another mirthless laugh

Pip Certainly not. What a phrase.
Henderson Don't you like it? You should do. It's yours.

Act II, Scene 1   39

Pip Is it?
Henderson You said that at a recent press conference, when you were discussing my possible departure, "If the Prime Minister should seek the sunny uplands of retirement".
Pip If ... Prime Minister. I also said you had many good years left — and a vital contribution to make.
Henderson And? Go on.
Pip (*after a hesitation*) "And as long as the Prime Minister remains in good health ..."
Henderson (*sharply*) That's it?
Pip What?
Henderson Health! Why is it that whenever there's an interview my health becomes a subject for discussion?
Pip I've no idea. I was merely responding to the question. (*Pause*) There's nothing wrong, is there?
Henderson No! (*He hesitates*) Just a little trouble with the waterworks — nothing uncommon in that.
Pip Not at all — I usually have to get out in the night and I'm half —— (*Quickly*) And there's nothing else we should worry about!
Henderson (*after a pause*) Well, there is a slight murmur ...
Pip A murmur perfectly acceptable in a man ...
Henderson Of my age?
Pip In a man who has given so much.
Henderson That's another thing that seems to crop up at interviews — my age. Do you know why?
Pip I've no idea. I never think of you as old.
Henderson Perhaps that's because I'm not.
Pip I think it's all mere speculation. Are you comfortable, John? Would you like another cushion?
Henderson No. Perhaps they wouldn't speculate quite so much if you weren't all so damned solicitous.
Pip If we appear solicitous, John, it's because we need you.
Henderson Do you? Did you see the recent poll?
Pip (*innocently*) Poll?
Henderson Apparently I'm the most unpopular Prime Minister of the last thirty years.
Pip Fifty.
Henderson So you have seen it. And why do you think that is?
Pip I don't know.
Henderson Don't you? You're at Prime Minister's question time. You've seen the behaviour of the front bench. They're like a bunch of unruly schoolboys. Slouching, hands in pockets, half asleep, doing crosswords, talking amongst themselves, planning holidays; anything sooner than listen to me.

Pip I hope you don't include me in that criticism, John.
Henderson No, Philip, I have to say you always listen to me in rapt attention. But the others: if my own front bench aren't prepared to listen to me — why should the Opposition?
Pip Indeed.
Henderson I'm being constantly undermined.
Pip I'll have a word with them. And I'll try and find out who's starting these rumours regarding your health.
Henderson There's no need. I think I know.
Pip You do?
Henderson I think it's Patch.
Pip Patch?
Henderson Berryman.
Pip (*quickly*) He's not wearing it.
Henderson (*staring*) How do you know?
Pip That's what I've heard.
Henderson (*after a pause*) You haven't seen him recently … ?
Pip No.

Henderson picks up the cigar discarded by Berryman and examines it thoughtfully

Henderson No, why should you? It's just that I heard he was downstairs — in the bar.
Pip Really?

Pip picks up the cigar and attempts to light it

Henderson The genie is out of the bottle again. I think he intends to challenge for the leadership.
Pip That's preposterous.
Henderson Is it? I've been watching him. He's been running around the House like an excited bridegroom.
Pip But it's laughable.
Henderson It may be laughable but unfortunately Berryman has this sense of destiny. It makes him difficult. What he doesn't realize is everyone else has it too. Even you, Philip
Pip But the party wouldn't accept him.
Henderson No, unless he had the right support. I hear the bridegroom's looking for a best man, Philip.
Pip Best man?
Henderson And a little bird told me it may be you.
Pip Good heavens! Why me?

Act II, Scene 1

Henderson Your standing's very high at the moment. Your speeches are much admired. Your braces are the talk of the media. Your bowler hat in the age of bare-headed men can't help but make you conspicuous. Rory Bremner has even impersonated you.
Pip I hope you don't think I'm trying to be noticed, Prime Minister.
Henderson Well, you've always been a model of self-effacement ...
Pip Let me assure you — with my hand on my heart — that I'd never support Berryman for Prime Minister.
Henderson I'm relieved to hear you say that. Of course your loyalty is beyond question. But it makes my request easier to make. I want you to put the genie back in the bottle.
Pip I don't understand.
Henderson Get rid of Berryman. I want him off the front bench — and out of the House. Offer him something if necessary — but he has to go.
Pip But suppose he doesn't want to go? He's very popular.
Henderson He's a war hero — they're always popular. But he'll go. There's something on him.
Pip What!
Henderson If he won't go willingly, tell him we'll withdraw the whip and he'll be deselected.
Pip You know something to his discredit?
Henderson I don't know all the facts. I find these things distasteful. Reynolds has the details. He had them from Special Branch. Have a word with him. All I know is that if it got out it could embarrass the government.
Pip (*appalled*) You mean Reynolds knows something about Berryman — some scandal? But why didn't he say something to me?
Henderson He couldn't. He had to be discreet. He is the Home Secretary — and it is privileged information. I don't know why you're so surprised. There's not much difference between naked ambition and naked lust, it's just that politicians have to choose one or the other. Berryman obviously got them confused.
Pip My God.

During the following, Lorna emerges tearfully from the bathroom

Henderson I can see I've shocked you. You've always been such a paragon of restraint, Philip. But I'm sure you feel that a minister who has compromised himself in this way should resign ...
Pip I entirely agree ... (*His voice dies away as he sees Lorna*)
Henderson I have no sympathy for a man who behaves dishonourably in private life and yet maintains an air of public respectability.
Pip (*faintly*) Well said, Prime Minister.

Lorna gives Pip a tragic, despairing look over Henderson's shoulder and exits, slamming the door

Henderson (*starting*) What was that?
Pip Er, security — checking up. My bodyguard's very concerned for my safety.
Henderson (*surprised*) You have a bodyguard?
Pip Yes.
Henderson But we already have men on.
Pip I know, but ——
Henderson No, I don't think you need a personal bodyguard. Security costs enough as it is.
Pip But I've had death threats.
Henderson We all have those, Philip. I'll speak to Reynolds — we really should have him withdrawn. After all, it's not as if you're Prime Minister.
Pip No, that's true.
Henderson (*rising*) Now I must go — I have to see Coupland.
Pip (*uneasily*) Coupland?
Henderson It's a bore but he says it's urgent and I don't like to put him off. His paper has been my greatest supporter of late. (*He turns*) And don't forget Berryman.
Pip I won't.

Pip escorts Henderson to the door

Henderson Good-night, Philip.
Pip Good-night, John.

Berryman stirs

Vicky darts out of the bedroom and into the lounge. She sees Pip and Henderson by the door and ducks into the closet

Pip sees Vicky out of the corner of his eye and keeps Henderson firmly turned towards the door

Henderson (*after a hesitation*) My rooms are below these, are they not?
Pip Yes. I hope I haven't been disturbing you.
Henderson Well, I have this very elegant chandelier — ornate and cut-glass. A short time ago it began swaying and tinkling in the most alarming manner — almost as if the earth was shaking. Did you have a similar experience — of the earth shaking?
Pip No. But I have been doing some pacing.

Act II, Scene 2   43

Henderson No, this was more than pacing. (*He shakes his head*) Strange. Good-night.

Henderson exits

Pip breathes a sigh of relief and crosses to the closet. He opens the door

There is an urgent tap at the outer door

Pip shuts the closet door abruptly, moves to the outer door and opens it

Reynolds enters

Reynolds Did I see the Prime Minister just leave?
Pip Yes.
Reynolds Was he suspicious?
Pip I'm not sure.
Reynolds Where's Berryman?
Pip In my bedroom. Dead drunk.
Reynolds Bloody hell! That's the worst thing that could have happened.
Pip No, it's not the worst thing that could have happened.
Reynolds What do you mean?
Pip Can I trust you?
Reynolds Of course you can trust me. We're in this together. What is it? (*He listens to the following in blank astonishment*)
Pip I'm going to lower my voice now, George. (*He does*) Berryman isn't the only problem. There's a girl in the closet wearing my shirt. I met her at an embassy reception. She may be a thrush — or was it a swallow? She's also an actress. She's at the Pier Theatre in "Run for your Knickers". Unfortunately Miss Fiske discovered her in my shirt and now she's hysterically jealous — possibly suicidal. Now Berryman was in bed with both of them but I don't know how much he'll remember. I think the PM may also suspect something — he's concerned about his chandelier ... I think that's about it ...

Reynolds laughs for a moment in disbelief, then realizes that Pip is not smiling. Reynolds opens the closet door, looks in and then closes it abruptly

Reynolds There's a girl in the closet wearing your shirt.
Pip That's what I said.
Reynolds Let me get this straight. You met this girl — who looks strangely like Miss Smart of the Christian Family Journal ——
Pip She is, but she's really an actress.

Reynolds You met an actress — at a foreign embassy — who is appearing in a play called "Run for your Knickers". You bring her back here.
Pip I didn't bring her back here.
Reynolds She gets into your shirt.
Pip Yes.
Reynolds Then you take her to bed along with Miss Fiske and Lionel Berryman.
Pip Not all at the same time.
Reynolds In a bed directly above where the Prime Minister's sleeping. I'm amazed at you, Pip. You haven't just fallen from grace — you've jumped with both feet.
Pip I don't know what came over me. What are we going to do?
Reynolds I suppose we'll have to try a little damage limitation. I find money's the answer in these cases.

Reynolds taps gently on the closet door and then opens it

Vicky steps out of the closet

Now my dear, before you go I'd like to discuss an arrangement for your future welfare ...
Vicky You mean money.
Reynolds Did I say that? No — I don't think that word need sully our lips. I am aware of the delicacy of your position.
Vicky Don't you mean your position?
Reynolds (*taking a pen and paper from the desk*) Now I'm going to ask you to write a figure on this piece of paper — bearing in mind that Mr Conway, though a wealthy man, hasn't unlimited resources. Say a figure that will compensate you for hopes dashed and expectations unfulfilled. A figure that will provide for a comfortable but not luxurious future. Just write it down ...
Vicky (*smiling*) Certainly. (*She writes a figure down and hands the paper back to Reynolds*)

Reynolds stares and his mouth drops open

Reynolds There must be some mistake. This says a million.
Vicky Yes.
Reynolds A million!
Vicky I don't think that word need sully our lips. (*She turns on Pip*) I offered you love — and you offered me money. What price a broken heart, Pip?

Pip groans

Act II, Scene 1   45

Vicky turns towards the bathroom

Reynolds Where are you going?
Vicky I'm going to take a shower. I suddenly feel dirty.

Vicky exits into the bathroom

We hear the sound of the shower, continuing during the following

Pip (*despairingly*) She never stops doing that.
Reynolds You don't think her heart's really broken?
Pip If it is — it's going to be a bloody expensive repair.
Reynolds I mean is it just remotely possible that she feels some affection for you? (*He looks at Pip doubtfully*)
Pip (*nettled*) Well, it's not inconceivable, George.
Reynolds In that case, it may be the best hope we have. Keep her here while I have a word with Miss Fiske.
Pip What about Berryman?
Reynolds Keep him here until I get back.
Pip Suppose he remembers?
Reynolds He never remembers. Another million brain cells died tonight, Pip.
Pip But suppose he does?

Reynolds moves towards the door

You've got something on him, haven't you?
Reynolds (*turning*) Who told you that?
Pip The PM ...
Reynolds Who told him?
Pip You did.
Reynolds Oh yes.
Pip Something scandalous?
Reynolds Yes.
Pip I don't understand; why did you suggest Berryman as a running mate if he was in disgrace?
Reynolds (*sighing*) Pip, in this day and age no-one can bear investigation. I couldn't find anyone spotless. I thought you were spotless and look what's happened. Say to any man I know your secret and he'll turn pale and leave the room.
Pip What's Berryman's secret?
Reynolds It's highly classified. (*Pause*) I'm going to speak to you in French, Pip.

Pip Don't, George.
Reynolds Why not?
Pip I won't understand you. Just lower your voice.
Reynolds Very well. (*He lowers his voice*) Special Branch has something on his file.
Pip They have a file on Berryman?
Reynolds They have a file on everyone. Even me. When I was made Home Secretary I asked to see mine.
Pip And did you?
Reynolds No, the blighters said they'd lost it. God knows what it says.
Pip What does Berryman's file say?
Reynolds It was some years ago, early one spring evening, shortly after his fall from grace. He was being watched as a potential security risk. Apparently earlier that evening he'd visited a massage parlour in Soho; stimulated by the experience he took a stroll through Hyde Park — and there, in fading light, committed an offence on a visiting Swedish businesswoman.
Pip What sort of offence?
Reynolds (*after a pause*) I believe he exposed himself.
Pip Good Lord.
Reynolds Whatever he did — she was badly shocked. And as you know the Swedes don't shock easily. She called for help. Berryman was detained and would have been charged but for the presence of a Special Branch officer who played his Monopoly card and got him out of jail. Berryman was freed but the complaint is still on the file. Her name was Ingrid Gustafson. I'm sure she could be produced — if necessary.
Pip Ingrid Gustafson.
Reynolds Don't use it unless you have to. You know what he's like. Now I must see Miss Fiske — see if I can talk her round. (*He opens the door*)
Pip (*curiously*) George — do you have a secret?
George Yes.
Pip What is it?
Reynolds (*after a pause*) If I told you, Pip, it wouldn't — be a secret ...

Reynolds exits

Pip returns to the bathroom door. He taps on it

Pip Vicky ... (*He listens at the door*)

During the following, the shower sound ends

  Higgs enters

Act II, Scene 1   47

(*Turning to Higgs*) Where are her clothes, Higgs?
Higgs Still checking.
Pip Did you find anything?
Higgs (*shrugging*) She shops at Marks and Spencer's.
Pip Not for much longer.

Higgs settles down and helps himself to strawberries

Higgs Did I see the Prime Minister leaving?
Pip Yes.
Higgs What did he want at this time of night?
Pip He was worried about his chandelier.
Higgs What?
Pip I don't know why he came so late. It could have waited until morning.
Higgs Makes you wonder if he knows something. That he's been tipped off. That there's somebody behind all this — some eminence greasy at work.
Pip Yes ... (*He studies Higgs for a moment, then joins him at the table and loads Higgs' plate further with strawberries*) My, you do have a wonderful appetite, don't you? (*Pause*) Higgs, I'm going to ask you something I never asked you before; it didn't seem important, now it seems critical. Who do you vote for?
Higgs The government.
Pip (*relieved*) Good. Then you're one of us.
Higgs No, I vote for the government.
Pip But we are the government.
Higgs I know. But if you weren't the government I wouldn't vote for you.
Pip You mean you always vote for the party in power?
Higgs Yes. I believe in the status quo. It's what I'm paid to uphold.
Pip But things would never change.
Higgs So what? I've never known things change for the better.
Pip Oh. (*Pause*) So at the moment you're one of us?
Higgs Right.
Pip We're in this together.
Higgs Emphatically.
Pip And none of this is going in the note-book?
Higgs No. (*He stares uncomprehendingly at Pip between mouthfuls during the following*)
Pip Good. You see I'm not trying to justify what's happened. (*He loads Higgs's plate further*) But a moment of weakness shouldn't invalidate years of public service — the good I can do. Look upon me, if you will, as a whisky priest who brings people to God though he himself is tarnished. Do you understand, Higgs?
Higgs You mean you drink as well?

Pip No! It's a metaphor. (*Impatiently*) Don't you know what a metaphor is?
Higgs (*doubtfully*) A metaphor?
Pip I thought you had to pass exams in the police force.
Higgs You do. That's why I never got beyond Sergeant. I was held back by metaphors. You need all those things these days. Size doesn't matter any more. That's why most senior officers are incredibly short.
Pip You don't approve of that?
Higgs No, and when we get into power, we'll get back to the six foot requirement and no beards. Bigger prisons and longer sentences.
Pip (*staring, appalled*) Higgs, you said when we get into power. Do you think you could rephrase that?
Higgs Sorry. *If* we get into power.
Pip You and me, Higgs?
Higgs We're in this together. I always thought there was more to my life than being a human shield. I've always had this feeling.
Pip (*sighing*) It's destiny, Higgs.
Higgs That's right — destiny.

Berryman opens the bedroom door and regards Pip suspiciously

Pip (*looking up and seeing Berryman*) Would you excuse us — Higgs?

Higgs hesitates, then picks up his bowl of strawberries and saunters out

Another malt, Lionel?
Berryman No, I must keep a clear head. Tomorrow, or I should say today, I'll take my traditional early morning swim — attended by the press. You can hold my towel. You'll be doing a great deal of that in the future. At the same time I shall announce my intention of challenging for the leadership.
Pip What makes you think I'll hold your towel?
Berryman (*trying the bathroom door*) Because there's a woman in your bathroom who is not your wife. And because I woke up in bed with her and your secretary. I thought I'd died and gone to heaven, Pip. I never had you down for a poodle faker. And now you're mine. (*He moves to the french windows and opens the curtains*) There's a new day dawning — and it's dawning for me.
Pip Do come away from that window, Lionel.
Berryman (*turning*) Don't worry, Pip. No-one's going to shoot me. I'd know if I was in someone's sights. It's a feeling you get when you've been in action. The trouble is you've never been under fire. You haven't the stomach for this, have you? If our positions had been reversed do you think I'd have warned you about the window? You're not ruthless enough.
Pip I'm learning, Lionel... Let me ask you something. Does the name Ingrid Gustafson mean anything to you?

Act II, Scene 1

Berryman slowly lights a cigar

Berryman Ingrid …?
Pip Gustafson.
Berryman (*after a pause*) Who told you?
Pip Reynolds.
Berryman I knew I couldn't trust him. I was answering a call of nature, Pip. It was a vile slander.
Pip Not according to Special Branch.
Berryman (*slowly*) It was a long time ago. Where is she now? Do you know?
Pip She could be found.
Berryman You can't be sure of that. But I can be sure of finding the girl in the bathroom. A bird in the hand. I have the advantage, Pip.
Pip But would you risk it?
Berryman Yes. I'm prepared to gamble, you're not.
Pip But I am.
Berryman Then I'll spin you for Prime Minister. (*He puts the cigar in the ashtray and produces a coin*)
Pip What?
Berryman You said you were prepared to gamble. Heads or tails? Come on, Pip. You have an even chance. You have no chance at all if I talk. (*He spins the coin and catches it*)
Pip (*after a hesitation*) Heads.
Berryman (*revealing the coin*) Bad luck. But I could have told you. It's destiny, Pip, destiny. Don't look so downhearted. Have a cigar. After all, we need each other, Pip. (*He gives Pip a cigar and lights it*) We're both in the same predicament. We both have a drawback. We're like two one-legged men at an arse-kicking contest. We need to support each other or we won't stand a chance.
Pip It seems I'm the one who's doing the supporting.
Berryman But you'll succeed me. You're my deputy.
Pip I was deputy before!
Berryman Then I'll make you Foreign Secretary as well. I don't think I've promised that to anyone. You can't be Chancellor — I've promised that to three people already. Foreign Secretary, Pip. Unlimited first-class travel and a permanent suntan. And you can take her with you. What do you say?
Pip I don't seem to have much choice.
Berryman Good man. (*He pats Pip on the back*)

Higgs enters

Higgs The Prime Minister's on his way.
Pip He can't find you here!

Pip bundles Berryman into the closet

Right, Higgs!

Higgs opens the door

Pip sees Berryman's cigar smoking in the ashtray, picks it up and hurls it into the closet. During the following, smoke creeps out under the closet door

Henderson enters

Higgs, a chair for the Prime Minister.
Henderson (*sharply*) I don't need a chair.

Higgs edges towards the exit

(*Shaking his head in Higgs's direction*) A needless expense, Philip.

Higgs exits, looking perturbed

Pip What is it, Prime Minister?
Henderson Sorry to disturb you yet again, Philip. But it's your speech for tomorrow, I wonder if I could have sight of it?
Pip Sight of it?
Henderson I thought it might be a good idea, under the circumstances …
Pip What circumstances?
Henderson So that I'd know how to respond.
Pip It's on the desk. Perhaps you'd like to take it away with you.
Henderson Thank you. (*He moves to the desk. He picks up the speech and then a spare sheet of paper. Looking at the paper*) What's this?
Pip (*hastily*) That's just a doodle.
Henderson A doodle. May I? (*Reading*) "I stand before you today mindful of the heavy responsibility so unexpectedly thrust upon me, yet with a sense of optimism." (*He pauses. Glancing at Pip*) "We have lost a great leader but not his legacy … " (*Drily*) Well, that's a relief.

Pip sees the smoke

Pip (*uncomfortably*) One has to provide for every eventuality …
Henderson Indeed. And it's not every day one reads one's own obituary. "A great leader".
Pip You were — I mean you are.
Henderson Philip, do you really think I lead this party? I mean like a general

Act II, Scene 1 51

leads his army? No. I lead this party like a fox. A fox, a few paces ahead of the pack, with one eye over his shoulder, scenting danger, and straining every sinew.

Berryman coughs faintly in the closet

Will you tell Berryman to come out of the closet before he chokes to death?

Pip opens the door of the closet

Berryman emerges in a cloud of smoke

Berryman Prime Minister.
Henderson Berryman! What are you doing here?
Berryman (*uneasily*) Just passing through.
Henderson That would seem more convincing if you weren't hiding in the closet. Or did you go in there to enjoy your cigar ——

Berryman is silent

Nothing to say? And you're normally so talkative. Should I tell you why you're here? You're here to conspire. What am I to make of this, Philip? You're my right hand.
Berryman I was your right hand once.
Henderson Yes, and I cut my right hand off because it offended.
Berryman Well, now it's your turn.
Pip Lionel!
Berryman You've no support left. You're finished.
Pip I don't think Lionel means finished exactly ...
Henderson Oh, I think Berryman knows what he means. But it doesn't really matter. I know your secret, Berryman.
Berryman What?
Henderson Reynolds said you'd go pale.
Berryman What secret?
Henderson Ingrid Gustafson.
Berryman That old slander. Prove it. She wouldn't say anything — even if you could find her.
Henderson But we have found her — and she's signed a statement.
Berryman What!
Henderson Reynolds has it. So you see, it's not me who's finished — it's you. Now I must visit the bathroom. It must be too much excitement.
Pip John, I ——

Henderson opens the bathroom door

Pip is surprised that the bathroom door is unlocked

Vicky edges from the bathroom into the bedroom

Henderson enters the bathroom

Berryman (*darkly*) The prostate. (*He moves to the bathroom door*)

Pip follows Berryman

(*Listening at the door*) Can't hear anything. Waiting for inspiration. "Too much excitement …"
Pip What?
Berryman That's what he said — too much excitement.

Vicky edges out of the bedroom and into the lounge. She slips unseen into the closet

Henderson opens the door into the bedroom. He looks around carefully and then withdraws

Pip What are you getting at?
Berryman If it's true about the prostate, it could be true about the heart. Tricky things, hearts. Any sudden shock. Not even that. Friend of mine bent down to pick up his credit cards — out like a light …
Pip What are you saying?
Berryman We've got to get him before he gets us.
Pip No. Let me speak to him. I'm sure we can sort things out.
Berryman It's too late. Can't you see — we've been stitched up. Where do you think Reynolds went when he left here?
Pip He went to see Miss Fiske — to talk to her.
Berryman No, he went straight to the Prime Minister. He's jumped ship — if he was ever on board in the first place. I said we couldn't trust him. He was always jealous of you, Pip. He couldn't wait to take your place with the Prime Minister. Who arranged our meeting this evening? He did.
Pip That's true. And he sent for my wife.
Berryman He probably even arranged for you to meet that girl.
Pip And he asked me to keep everyone here.
Berryman So Henderson would discover you in your true colours. (*He pauses*) Listen for the flush. (*He moves to the sofa*)
Pip What are you going to do?
Berryman I'm going to try a long shot.
Pip What long shot?

Act II, Scene 1

Berryman (*fiercely*) Just listen for the flush!

The toilet flushes, off

Pip (*listening*) He's flushing.

Berryman takes a firework from his pocket, lights it from his cigar and slips it under the sofa

Henderson emerges from the bathroom. He regards Pip and Berryman suspiciously

Henderson Still here, Berryman.
Berryman Just want to say something before I go (*He motions to the sofa*)

Henderson sits. Pip and Berryman sit; Pip looks faintly bewildered

Do you know what you are, Henderson? A dinosaur — a political dinosaur. And while you've had your head in the trees, chewing at the succulent leaves of power, men have been busy digging pits ...

We hear the hiss of the firework

You're extinct, Henderson, and like the dinosaur you've failed to see it — but unlike the dinosaur you're going to go out with a bang — a big bang ...

There is a deafening explosion

Pip and Berryman look at Henderson. Henderson's face freezes in shock. Berryman gives a long, low chuckle. Then slowly his smile fades and he looks faintly perturbed. He slips out of his chair on to the carpet and lies motionless. Henderson and Pip stare down at him

CURTAIN

SCENE 2

The same. Half an hour later

When the CURTAIN *rises, Pip is by the drinks cabinet, pouring himself a drink. Henderson stands looking out of the french windows, drink in hand*

An ambulance siren can be heard; it fades as the ambulance moves away

Henderson (*turning from the window*) There he goes.
Pip Yes.
Henderson A tragedy.
Pip Indeed.
Henderson Who'd have thought it. In the prime of life.
Pip Checked out by his doctor only this week and pronounced fit.
Henderson If we only knew. Did you hear his last words?
Pip Well, they were very faint but it sounded like, "Very well, I'll take the Foreign Office."
Henderson Yes, that's what I thought. A politician to the end. Sad to think that good eye is now as glazed as its fellow.
Pip Yes. But at least Ingrid Gustafson can't hurt him now.
Henderson Yes. I'll have to find something nice to say about him for tomorrow's papers.
Pip Yes, it'll be the big story.
Henderson Not quite the big story. You'll be the big story, Philip.
Pip Look, I don't know what Reynolds has been saying —
Henderson It wasn't Reynolds. He merely changed sides. Once he saw which way the wind was blowing.
Pip What wind?
Henderson Coupland came to see me this evening. He was concerned — or I should say his employer was concerned — for the good name of the party. Out of consideration for me they've deferred publishing certain revelations. But it's conditional. The condition is your resignation.
Pip They can't. They can't threaten me like this. They haven't any evidence.
Henderson Apparently they will have. Coupland is waiting for a phone call — and then the presses will begin to roll. It won't happen all at once; it'll take a few days — a few teasing articles — then a transcript of the tapes.
Pip Tapes?
Henderson And then finally the grainy pictures — not the finest quality but good enough to make the point.
Pip He's bluffing.
Henderson He seems very confident that he'll have all the evidence by tomorrow.
Pip He's lying. I won't resign.
Henderson Philip, what can I say? If you give me your word as a Member of the House and as a gentleman — bearing in mind that they're not necessarily the same thing — then I have no choice but to believe you.
Pip (*after a deep breath*) You have my word.

Vicky coughs faintly in the closet

Act II, Scene 2   55

Henderson Really?

Henderson opens the closet door

Vicky steps out of the closet. She is wearing Pip's bowler, tie and coat with pants, stockings and high heels beneath. She tips the bowler slightly over one eye. In a husky voice, she sings the first verse of "Falling in Love Again" in the manner of Marlene Dietrich

Pip stares incredulously. Henderson regards Vicky impassively

Vicky fondles Henderson's hair for a moment and sings the second verse. She takes a sip from his glass, dips her finger into its contents and touches Henderson's nose

Henderson remains unsmiling

Vicky continues; in a heavy German accent, she sings "Happy Birthday" to Henderson, but calls him "Mr Conway". She kisses Henderson

Henderson remains impassive

Henderson I'm not Mr Conway. That is Mr Conway — and his birthday is in April.
Vicky April! Then there must be some terrible mistake.
Henderson Yes.
Vicky The kissogram was definitely ordered for tonight.
Henderson You're a kissogram?
Vicky Himmel, do you think I normally walk around like this?

Pip groans silently

The instructions were very clear. A birthday celebration for this evening — stressing time and place. It was from the Home Secretary himself.
Henderson (*staring*) Reynolds?
Vicky (*putting her hand to her lips*) Unless ... Could it be an attempt to embarrass Mr Conway? It does happen — someone with a grudge. *Mein Gott!*
Henderson I think you'd better get dressed, my dear.
Vicky (*bowing*) Your Excellency.

Vicky exits into the bathroom

Henderson regards Pip, who grins sheepishly

Henderson Well, whatever next.
Pip Yes.
Henderson I'll expect your resignation in the morning, giving personal reasons — possibly family pressures. (*He smiles faintly*) I'm sure there'll be some. No, wait a moment — why not ill health? Just something I can show the cabinet — and Coupland. And I'll send you a nice letter back thanking you for your sterling service.
Pip But you heard what she said ...
Henderson It was a nice try. And I enjoyed the performance. But it's too late, Philip. The cat is out of the bag. Funny, I never thought that was your particular weakness. One lives and learns. The strange thing is I thought my race was run. The tape was fading from my sight — the strength was draining from my legs. I was almost ready to hand over the baton ...
Pip I know — that's what I thought. All I did was hold out my hand.
Henderson No — you snatched for it, Philip. That was your mistake. But you did me a favour. I didn't think I wanted it any more until you tried to take it away. Now I feel restored — fitter than I've been in years.
Pip But I can still be of service — the party needs me.
Henderson No. The party doesn't need you, Philip. It doesn't need me. We, unfortunately, need the party. You'll soon be forgotten. Like those rockets out there — a fierce blaze of colour and then down to earth.

There is a knock on the door

Reynolds enters

Reynolds (*looking uneasily at Philip*) Oh, Prime Minister, Coupland wishes to make his farewells. He's expecting a phone call.
Henderson Ah, the phone call. Well, we mustn't keep the press waiting. Stay behind after Coupland's gone, George. I'd like to discuss the deputy leadership with you.
Reynolds The deputy leadership. I'm overwhelmed, Prime Minister.
Henderson Are you? (*He smiles*) Well, I'm sure you won't be overwhelmed for long, George.

Reynolds and Henderson exit

Vicky emerges from the bathroom

Vicky (*looking sympathetically at Pip*) That's torn it.
Pip Torn it is something of an understatement.

Higgs enters carrying the holdall. He looks deeply serious

Act II, Scene 2

Higgs I've brought the clothes.
Pip Too late I'm afraid.
Higgs I'd have come sooner but I was detained. (*He puts the holdall down*) I don't know how to put this ...
Pip What's the matter, Higgs?
Higgs It's your wife.
Pip (*alarmed*) She's not here, is she?
Higgs No. (*Pause*) It's the policeman's lot I suppose but I never get used to it.
Pip Get used to what?
Higgs I find a drink usually helps in these circumstances.
Pip Well, have one.
Higgs I mean you. (*He pours Pip a drink*)
Pip For God's sake — what is it?
Higgs It was from your local hunt. They asked me to pass it on. There's been an accident.
Pip Accident. Where?
Higgs In the hunting field. Apparently your wife was last seen earlier in the day trying to clear a high fence. She was making a third attempt and the horse was under the whip. They didn't find her until this evening when they saw the boots.
Pip Boots?
Higgs Excuse me. This is the bit I find difficult ... (*He takes a sip from the drink he's poured for Pip*) She was thrown into a heap of farmyard manure — only her boots were visible. Unfortunately it didn't break her fall ...
Pip You mean she's ...
Higgs Instantly.
Pip Poor Bunty.
Higgs She didn't suffer. It was a quick death — not clean but quick. And if it's any consolation, she cleared the fence.
Pip (*sadly*) She'd have liked that.
Higgs Don't fight it ... Let the tears flow — they usually help in these cases.
Pip Yes. (*He glances at Vicky*) I'm sure they'll come in a moment — it's the shock.
Vicky Wait a minute. When did this happen, Higgs?
Higgs Early this afternoon — from what we could ascertain.
Vicky Then we didn't!
Pip Didn't what?
Vicky We didn't commit adultery. We didn't do anything wrong. We're back in the Garden of Eden. We're blameless. You were a widower at the time.
Pip (*staring*) You're right, Vicky. I'm innocent, both in the eyes of church and state.

Higgs But you didn't know you were innocent.
Pip That's not the point. You're an expert in the law, Higgs. Did I do anything wrong?
Higgs Not technically — technically you were a free man.
Pip I'm respectable again.
Vicky Your reputation's unblemished.
Higgs There should have been a period of mourning.
Vicky He said he was respectable — he didn't say he was perfect.
Pip And we all have different ways of dealing with our grief, Higgs.
Higgs (*drily*) I can see you're made of sterner stuff than the rest of us.
Vicky Pip, if we've done nothing wrong — there's no reason for you to resign.

Pip looks hopeful for a moment and then shakes his head sadly

Pip It's too late — too many people know. Higgs for example.
Higgs I wouldn't use it against you, Pip. We're in this together. Although I would like a little less of the Higgs.
Pip What?
Higgs It's "Higgs, do this" and "Higgs, do that". And, "Wait outside, Higgs". My name does have a handle. Why don't you call me Brendan?
Pip (*staring*) Brendan? Why should I call you Brendan?
Higgs That's my name.
Pip I couldn't call you Brendan. What would people think? See what I mean, Vicky? How could I govern like that? And it's not just Higgs and the rest knowing. Coupland's waiting for a phone call — then he'll be in possession of pictures and tapes.
Higgs Pictures and tapes. I knew I should have had this place swept ... It's probably been bugged all along. (*He goes into the bedroom, switches on the main lights and searches for bugs*)
Vicky You could fight them, Pip.

Pip hands Vicky the holdall

Pip Put your clothes on, Vicky.
Vicky They could be bluffing. You could deny it.
Pip (*shaking his head*) No. One thing I've found out tonight. I'm a bad liar.

Vicky picks up the holdall, moves to the bathroom door and pauses

Vicky The trouble with you is you're a defeatist.

Vicky exits

Act II, Scene 2

Higgs (*bending over the carpet*) Hallo. What's this? This carpet's been tampered with ...

Pip joins Higgs in the bedroom

See? It's been recently joined together. (*He pulls back the carpet to reveal a shiny metal fitment attached to the floor*) Ah. See this fitment. How new and shiny it is? It's been recently fitted.
Pip What is it?
Higgs A listening device, I imagine. Situated where they'd hear everything — every creak and groan. No wonder they knew what was going on. Now, if I just unscrew this cap ... I think we'll find ... (*He unscrews the fitment*)

There is a flash, a loud crack, and the Lights in the bedroom go out

What was that?
Pip A short circuit. Apparently you've fused the lights — Brendan. (*He returns to the lounge*)
Higgs (*following*) Well, it was worth a try.

Pip turns and looks at Higgs thoughtfully

What are you looking at me like that for?
Pip I wonder if you're as stupid as you seem. You're the only one who has had access to this room. You seem to know everything that's going on. You're Special Branch and you have privileged information. You keep saying we're in this together but how do I know you're not going to make that phone call, Brendan?
Higgs (*shocked*) I wouldn't. I couldn't. Look, if you're looking for a suspect. There's someone a good deal closer to you than me. (*He glances at the bathroom door*) I'm referring to the lady of the night ...
Pip Vicky?
Higgs She could be your agent provocative. They had to have someone on the inside. I mean, what's in it for her? Why is she here if it's not for the money?
Pip (*after a hesitation*) She says she loves me.
Higgs (*chuckling*) Loves you. You don't believe that. When I was on the force I once encountered a man on the roof of the Midland Bank who said he was looking for a chiropodist. And that story's more likely than the one you've just come out with. She's in it for the money.
Pip All right. You've made your point. Now I suggest you go and report this lighting fault to the management — omitting, of course, your part in the proceedings.

Higgs Right. (*He moves to the door and pauses by it*) It could have been worse — could have been a bomb.
Pip (*wearily*) A bomb would have been a blessed release, Higgs.

Higgs exits

Pip stares at the closet for a moment. He opens the door and searches inside. He appears with Vicky's handbag. He moves to the desk and begins searching through the contents of the bag

Vicky emerges from the bathroom, half dressed, and watches Pip

Vicky What are you looking for?
Pip (*quietly*) These. (*He produces a small camera and a tape recorder from the bag*) It was a trap, wasn't it? A honey trap.
Vicky Yes.
Pip Why, Vicky? Did I deserve this?
Vicky No. But I hadn't worked in two years. They got me the job at the Pier Theatre. They can do anything.
Pip And how much are they paying you?
Vicky Nothing. That would be conspiracy — but they'll pay me a fortune for my story and the evidence.
Pip (*drily*) What price a broken heart, Vicky?
Vicky (*shrugging*) I knew it was a terrible line.
Pip Well, it appears that now I have the evidence. The camera and the tape recorder.
Vicky Why don't you examine them? You'll see they've not been used.
Pip What? (*He examines the camera and tape recorder*)
Vicky I'm not going to make that phone call. You're in the clear.
Pip Am I? They know you're here. What were you supposed to be doing for the past couple of hours?
Vicky Posing as a journalist. And when I came on to you, you rebuffed me. That's the part they'll find hard to believe. But it's my story and I'm sticking to it.
Pip (*staring*) I don't understand. If you agreed to do this, why have you changed your mind?
Vicky Because I'm totally unreliable.
Pip But you said you were totally reliable.
Vicky Did I?
Pip Yes.
Vicky That just shows how totally unreliable I am. The trouble is I'm so easily bribed. I was the little girl who took sweets from strangers — imagine what I'd do for smoked salmon.

Act II, Scene 2

Pip (*smiling*) That's not the reason. Reynolds was right: you're the best hope I have — my first piece of luck. (*He kisses her*)
Vicky Then why don't you fight?
Pip It's too late. The Prime Minister saw you in my shirt.
Vicky It would be your word against his.
Pip But he's the Prime Minister.
Vicky Suppose you were the Prime Minister?
Pip It's not going to happen, Vicky.
Vicky How do you know? Perhaps it's your —
Pip Don't say it.
Vicky Destiny. Why not? Perhaps you were meant to be Prime Minister.

A siren sounds

Pip and Vicky move to the french windows

Pip (*looking alarmed*) An ambulance! It's not Berryman, is it? He hasn't recovered. They're not bringing him back!
Vicky No. It's come to fetch someone. Probably an accident with a firework.

Lorna enters. She regards Pip and Vicky with a wild stare

I'd better finish getting dressed.

Vicky exits into the bathroom

Pip (*uneasily*) Are you all right, Lorna?
Lorna I've just heard ... Isn't it terrible?
Pip (*sadly*) Did Higgs tell you?
Lorna It's all round the building. Two deaths in twenty-four hours — it's ghastly.
Pip I know.
Lorna There's such a wave of sympathy, Pip.
Pip Thank you. It was a shock.
Lorna (*studying Pip*) How do you feel now?
Pip Well, Berryman wasn't a close friend but she was very dear to me ...
Lorna (*staring*) She? I was talking about the Prime Minister.
Pip What about the Prime Minister?
Lorna He's dead.
Pip Dead! When? Where?
Lorna A few minutes ago — downstairs.
Pip My God! It must have been delayed shock. So it finally got him.
Lorna What?

Pip His heart. The stories were true.
Lorna No, it wasn't his heart — it was a chandelier.
Pip (*incredulously*) Chandelier?
Lorna Right on top of him. They say it started to tinkle and sway, and he stood underneath it staring up — and then for some inexplicable reason it came crashing down on top of him. He died instantly.
Pip I can't believe it. (*He moves to the bedroom door. He looks in, checking the lie of the carpet, then closes the door gently*) A chance in a million.
Lorna Yes. Pip — you said *she*. Who were you talking about?
Pip Bunty: she was killed in a riding accident — around lunchtime.
Lorna I can't believe it.
Pip They say these things go in threes.
Lorna That's terrible.
Pip Yes.
Lorna Although it's not as if you were sleeping together.
Pip True.
Lorna And she died with her boots on.
Pip Yes, that's how they found her. They saw her boots.
Lorna It's the way she'd have wanted to go.
Pip Yes ... Well, possibly not the manure but ——
Lorna Manure?
Pip Now I want you to order a car. I must be at the Palace by tomorrow morning. Oh, and try and raise the Chief Whip. (*He takes a bag from the closet*)
Lorna But, Pip — do you know what this means?
Pip Yes. I'm Prime Minister.
Lorna No, it means you're free.
Pip (*busily packing his bag*) Well, yes — that as well.
Lorna And I forgive you.
Pip Thank you. You'd better pack a bag as well — there's not much time.
Lorna Pip, doesn't Bunty's death mean anything? All you can think about is being Prime Minister.
Pip Lorna, Bunty's been dead since lunch time; I've been Prime Minister for five minutes — let me get used to it. Get hold of the Lord Chancellor — I want advice on the constitutional position. I think the last time a Prime Minister died in office was when someone shot Perceval — there's no modern precedent. I must kiss hands and be the man in possession. Hurry.
Lorna (*firmly*) No.
Pip What?

Lorna puts her arms around Pip and holds him close

Lorna You promised that if you were free we'd be together.
Pip Did I?

Act II, Scene 2   63

Lorna You never meant it, did you? Just as long as I kept writing your speeches.
Pip Lorna, it was more that you *assumed* we'd be together.
Lorna I'm not letting you go, Pip.
Pip Aren't you?
Lorna You know I could ruin you, don't you?
Pip What?
Lorna I only have to start talking and you're finished.
Pip You think so?
Lorna Yes, and I will.
Pip (*smiling*) You won't.
Lorna You think not?
Pip Yes. And do you know why? Because I'm going to give you something you've always wanted. Something better than marriage. A safe seat ...
Lorna (*relaxing her grip slightly*) I've heard that before. How long do I have to wait?
Pip You don't have to wait. Two have just become vacant ... Take your pick. The Prime Minister had a majority of twenty thousand ...
Lorna But the Prime Minister's barely cold.
Pip Cold enough ...
Lorna (*relaxing her grip further*) You'd put me forward?
Pip I'm Prime Minister — it's within my gift. Of course, I couldn't do it if we were married — it would smack of nepotism.
Lorna Quite.

Lorna now holds only Pip's hands

Pip So you have to make a choice. Think of it. The Right Honourable Lorna Fiske MP. How proud your parents would be ...

Lorna slowly releases Pip's hands

   The Right Honourable Lorna Fiske MP. Secretary of State for the Treasury ...
Lorna I'll pack a bag.

Lorna exits

Pip returns to his packing

Higgs enters

Higgs What's all the fuss about? Ambulance, sirens, people weeping. What's going on?

Pip Don't you know? The Prime Minister's dead.
Higgs Blimey!
Pip And do you know how he died? He was crushed by a falling chandelier. (*He looks toward the bedroom*)
Higgs (*following Pip's gaze*) Whoops.
Pip Yes, whoops. You, the very person who was supposed to give his life to protect the first man of the kingdom and you bring him down with a chandelier.
Higgs My God!
Pip Of course I shall do my best to keep this between ourselves.
Higgs I don't suppose they'll think it was international terrorism?
Pip No — I don't think international terrorists have ever used the chandelier as a weapon. If this ever got out your career would be — what was it? — in tatters.
Higgs Yes, sir.
Pip So I'll do my best to keep you out of it.
Higgs Can you do that?
Pip Of course I can — I'm Prime Minister. And as Prime Minister I'll need more protection. Arrange for Mr Henderson's men to join our party. We're leaving in a few minutes.
Higgs Sir.
Pip (*smiling*) That's better. I like this return to the old servile manner, Higgs.
Higgs Yes, sir.

Higgs exits

Vicky emerges from the bathroom, slipping on her raincoat

Pip Are you leaving?
Vicky You bet I'm leaving. There are more deaths around here than in *Hamlet*. And I'm not waiting to play Ophelia. Besides, I've got a show to give and that requires stamina. You don't know what it's like at the end of the pier in October. Storm-tossed; drenched with spray; the smell of damp anoraks ... It's like performing in a lifeboat.
Pip Will I see you again?
Vicky (*surprised*) Do you want to see me again?
Pip Yes. Does that surprise you?
Vicky Yes — I usually fail the audition.
Pip Not this time.
Vicky (*after a pause*) I've turned down a lot of money. What are you offering?
Pip A world stage, Vicky.
Vicky Well, that beats the Pier Theatre. I could do it, Pip.

Act II, Scene 2

Pip Of course you could.
Vicky After all, it's only acting, isn't it?
Pip Reynolds says it's a beauty contest.
Vicky Then look no further. I'm so right for the part ...
Pip That's what I thought.

Pip and Vicky kiss

There is knock on the door

Vicky I'd better go while I can take advantage of the pandemonium ... (*She moves to the door, turning up the collar of her coat. She opens the door*)

Reynolds enters and looks uneasily at Pip

(*Smiling at Reynolds*) I think you've just made a bad career move.

Vicky exits

There is the sound of a siren

Pip regards Reynolds bleakly

Reynolds There goes the ambulance.
Pip Yes.
Reynolds Too late I'm afraid. But at least there was no suffering. He died almost at once. I tried giving him the kiss of life but it was useless.
Pip (*coldly*) I thought you said there was no suffering?
Reynolds I need a drink. (*He pours himself a drink and looks at Pip cautiously*) Here's to you, Pip.
Pip To me?
Reynolds The king is dead — long live the king. After all, there's no precedent for this. The party could insist on an election but we could head that off.
Pip Could we?
Reynolds (*looking into the bedroom at the carpet*) An election usually follows a resignation — quite what happens when the Prime Minister is struck down by a chandelier I don't know ... (*Referring to the bedroom floor*) Strange how that happened. A chance in a million.
Pip Yes.
Reynolds Pip, you know the PM promised me the deputy leadership?
Pip I had that impression.
Reynolds But after mature consideration I turned it down.

Pip Was that after the chandelier fell or before?
Reynolds Of course, I'd be perfectly happy to assume the position now.
Pip No, George — I wouldn't feel safe.
Reynolds Possibly the F.O. ...
Pip Sorry, George.
Reynolds Or even Chancellor.
Pip I think we need some fresh faces.
Reynolds Well, I could retain my present position for the time being.
Pip That's been promised.
Reynolds (*desperately*) Surely there's some way in which I can serve?
Pip I'm going to lower my voice now, George.
Reynolds Yes?
Pip After the way you've acted tonight ... I wouldn't put you in charge of the paper clips.
Reynolds But I gathered your support. I masterminded your campaign.
Pip Don't you mean your campaign?
Reynolds You can't drop me like this.
Pip I'm not dropping you, George. Have you thought about the Lords?
Reynolds (*shocked*) The Lords!
Pip I can see you haven't. Lord Reynolds — it does have a ring to it.

Higgs enters

Higgs The car's ready, sir.
Pip Thank you, Higgs.
Reynolds You can't send me there. You can't get rid of me that easily. I know about the chandelier. I know about the girl. I have access to files. I can make a good friend or a bad enemy.
Pip No, you make a bad friend and a bad enemy. Do your worst, George — you can't touch me. Are they cheering out there, Higgs?
Higgs Yes, sir — I think it's for the Prime Minister.
Pip I am the Prime Minister.
Higgs No, they're cheering the ambulance. He was never very popular.
Pip (*moving to the window*) Still, I think I'll give them a wave ——
Higgs I wouldn't.
Reynolds (*angrily*) You fool — do you think it's your destiny? Berryman thought that, and Henderson — and where are they now? Power comes from planning. Waiting and watching, seizing the opportunity. And from infinite patience — and that's what I have: patience. I can wait ... Pip.

Pip smiles back at him and waves from the french windows

Higgs (*urgently*) Come away from that window, sir! (*He snatches Pip's arm*)

Act II, Scene 2   67

There is the loud report of a rifle shot, almost deafening, louder than any firework. It is followed by the tinkling of glass. Pip and Higgs freeze in tableau

Reynolds stands motionless

Higgs (*after a long pause*) Are you all right, sir?

Pip slowly removes Higgs's hand from his arm

Pip Yes, Higgs.
Higgs Strewth! You must have lived right.
Pip No — it's destiny, Higgs.

   Pip exits

   Higgs picks up Pip's bag and follows

Reynolds stands motionless for a moment and then crumples slowly to the floor

CURTAIN

FURNITURE AND PROPERTY LIST

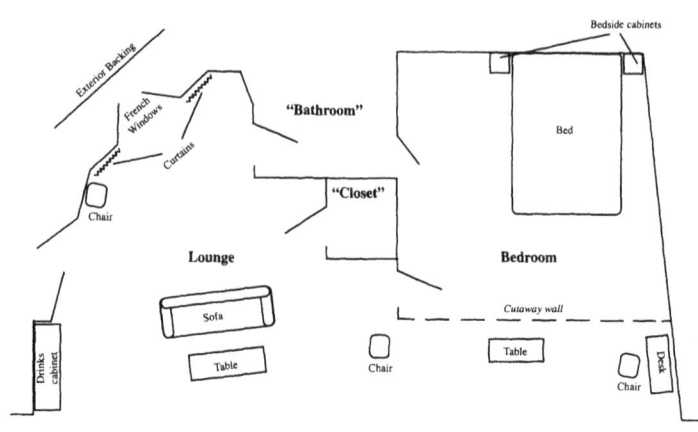

ACT I

Scene 1

On stage: LOUNGE
Sofa
Easy chair
Drinks cabinet with miniature bottles of spirits, glasses etc.
Two coffee tables. *On* DL *one*: ashtray
Vases of flowers, including roses
Desk. *On it*: papers, a form, magazines, telephone, pad of paper, pens
Upright desk chair
Dispatch box
"Do Not Disturb" sign — in three languages — on doorknob

CLOSET
Jacket for **Pip**
Trolley. *On it*: champagne, strawberries, sandwiches, napkins, glasses, plates, bowls, cutlery, etc.
Holdall
Handbag containing small camera and tape recorder
Bag

Furniture and Property List

BEDROOM
Divan bed
Two bedside tables. *On one*: radio
Under carpet: shiny metal fitment (removable)

Off stage: Sheaf of papers (**Lorna**)
Towel (**Vicky**)

Personal: **Pip**: Brussels sprout in top pocket, change in trousers pocket

SCENE 2

Set: **Vicky**'s clothes from ACT I, SCENE 1 scattered around lounge

Off stage: Glass of water (**Reynolds**)
Cigar and dummy firework (**Berryman**)

ACT II

SCENE 1

Personal: **Berryman**: cigar, lighter, coin, dummy firework

SCENE 2

No additional props

LIGHTING PLOT

Practicals required: table lamps
A lounge, with exterior backing beyond windows, a bedroom. The same throughout

ACT I, SCENE 1

To open: Lounge lit only by practical lamp with cover spot; bedroom unlit; exterior backing unlit, with occasional firework flash effect (continuous); bathroom lit

Cue 1 The outer door opens (Page 1)
Cut bathroom light

Cue 2 **Higgs** switches on the main lounge lights (Page 2)
Bring up full interior lights on lounge

Cue 3 **Higgs** switches off the main lounge lights (Page 3)
Cut full interior lights on lounge

Cue 4 **Higgs** switches on the main lounge lights (Page 3)
Bring up full interior lights on lounge

Cue 5 **Higgs** dims the lights (Page 5)
Dim lights

Cue 6 **Vicky** exits into the bathroom (Page 10)
Snap on bathroom light

Cue 7 **Vicky** puts her arms around **Pip** (Page 19)
Firework rocket effect on exterior backing

Cue 8 **Pip** turns **Vicky** so her back is to the french windows (Page 19)
Fade all lights; firework rocket effect on exterior backing

ACT I, SCENE 2

To open: Lounge lit only by practical lamp with cover spot; bedroom unlit; exterior backing unlit; bathroom lit

Cue 9 **Pip** switches on the main lounge light (Page 19)
Bring up full interior lights on lounge

Lighting Plot

Cue 10	**Vicky** switches lamps on and off *Flash bedside lamps with covering spot;* *see script p. 22*	(Page 22)
Cue 11	**Vicky** sits up and puts on a lamp *Bring up bedside lamp with covering spot*	(Page 36)
Cue 12	**Vicky** switches off the lamp *Cut bedside lamp*	(Page 36)
Cue 13	**Lorna** switches on the lamp *Bring up bedside lamp with covering spot*	(Page 36)
Cue 14	**Pip**:"Not at all, Prime Minister." *Fade to black-out*	(Page 37)

ACT II, SCENE 1

To open: Lounge fully lit; bedroom unlit; exterior backing unlit; bathroom lit

No cues

ACT II, SCENE 2

To open: Lounge fully lit; bedroom unlit; exterior backing unlit; bathroom lit

Cue 15	**Higgs** switches on the bedroom lights *Bring up lights on bedroom*	(Page 58)
Cue 17	**Higgs** unscrews the fitment *Flash, then bedroom lights go out*	(Page 59)

EFFECTS PLOT

ACT I

Cue 1	As the CURTAIN rises *Sounds of chanting, shouting mob and occasional explosion of firework (continuous)*	(Page 1)
Cue 2	**Vicky** exits into the bathroom *Sound of bath being run*	(Page 10)
Cue 3	**Pip**: "Higgs!" *Cut sound of bath being run*	(Page 12)
Cue 4	Firework rocket effect on exterior backing *Explosion of firework sound*	(Page 19)
Cue 5	Firework rocket effect on exterior backing *Explosion of firework sound; then fade firework and chanting sounds*	(Page 19)
Cue 6	**Vicky** accidentally switches on the radio *Burst of music*	(Page 22)
Cue 7	**Vicky** fiddles desperately with the radio switches *Volume increases, station changes several times*	(Page 22)
Cue 8	**Berryman** throws the firework out of the window *Loud bang, off*	(Page 32)

ACT II

Cue 9	**Vicky** exits into the bathroom *Sound of shower*	(Page 45)
Cue 10	**Pip** listens at the bathroom door *Cut shower sound during following dialogue*	(Page 46)
Cue 11	**Pip** hurls the cigar into the closet *Smoke creeps out under closet door*	(Page 50)
Cue 12	**Berryman**: "Just listen for the flush!" *Toilet flush*	(Page 53)

Effects Plot

Cue 13	**Berryman**: " … men have been busy digging pits …" *Hiss of firework*	(Page 53)
Cue 14	**Berryman**: "— a big bang ..." *Deafening explosion*	(Page 53)
Cue 15	As ACT II SCENE 2 begins *Ambulance siren, fading*	(Page 54)
Cue 16	**Higgs** unscrews the fitment. Flash *Loud crack*	(Page 59)
Cue 17	**Vicky**: "Perhaps you were meant to be Prime Minister." *Siren*	(Page 61)
Cue 18	**Vicky** exits *Siren*	(Page 65)
Cue 19	**Higgs** snatches **Pip's** arm *Loud report of rifle shot; tinkling of glass*	(Page 66)

www.ingramcontent.com/pod-product-compliance
Ingram Content Group UK Ltd.
Pitfield, Milton Keynes, MK11 3LW, UK
UKHW021846210426
53221PUK00022B/487